SPEARFISHING
FOR SKIN AND SCUBA DIVERS

BEST PUBLISHING COMPANY

SPEARFISHING
FOR SKIN AND SCUBA DIVERS

BY
STEVEN M. BARSKY

BEST PUBLISHING COMPANY

Photography by Steven M. Barsky, unless otherwise indicated.

Copyright © 1997 by Best Publishing Company.

Reprinted 2009 by Best Publishing Company.

All rights reserved

No part of this book may be reproduced, stored in a retrieval system, or transmitted in any form or by any means, electronic, mechanical, photocopying, microfilming, recording, or otherwise, without written permission from the publisher.

ISBN: 978-0-941332-59-0
Library of Congress catalog card number: 97-71104

Text design by Linda Longnaker.
Composed, printed and bound in the United States of America.

Best Publishing Company
2355 North Steves Boulevard
P.O. Box 30100
Flagstaff, Arizona 86003-0100 USA

WARNING

⚠ **WARNING:** Spearfishing, like any diving activity, is a potentially hazardous sport. However, unlike most other pieces of diving equipment, a speargun is a potentially lethal weapon. Spearguns can harm or kill you, and they can kill other divers, if you are careless. Before you engage in spearfishing you should receive training in spearfishing safety and techniques from a certified diving instructor. This manual is not a substitute for training in skin or scuba diving, or spearfishing.

TABLE OF CONTENTS

	Acknowledgements	ix
	Introduction	xi
Chapter 1	Spearfishing in Perspective	1
Chapter 2	Types of Spearfishing Gear	11
Chapter 3	Spearfishing Accessories	35
Chapter 4	Freediving Gear	53
Chapter 5	Where to Find Fish	63
Chapter 6	Types of Fish	75
Chapter 7	Developing Your Spearfishing Techniques	105
Chapter 8	Maximizing Your Freediving Abilities	121
Chapter 9	Spearfishing Competition	135
Chapter 10	The Future of Spearfishing	139
	Appendix	137
	Recommended reading	143
	About the author	144
	Index	145

Acknowledgements

Spearfishing is one of the most challenging of underwater activities. It is at least as difficult as underwater photography, if not more so. I've been fortunate to know some outstanding underwater hunters who have shared their secrets with me and provided invaluable information for this book. The best information comes from them, and any mistakes that remain in this book are my own.

Matt Lum is one of the truly great spearfishermen on the west coast. Like all people who are exceptionally good at what they do, Matt will share his information on diving techniques with anyone who is interested, yet he is extraordinarily modest. Matt has always been open with his information on free diving and has been kind enough to allow me to photograph him on numerous occasions. Matt reviewed the manuscript and made numerous suggestions for improvements.

Skip Dunham is a long time friend, an excellent diver, and an underwater sportsman. We have made countless dives together for hunting and photography and many of these dives are some of my fondest memories. Skip is a superior waterman and his information on gun building and hunting techniques have helped to enrich this book immeasurably. Skip also carefully reviewed the manuscript and gave valuable criticism.

Mark Perlstein, is a serious diver, and among the best underwater hunters. He has landed both yellowtail and white sea bass while hunting on scuba underwater, a feat that few can boast. Few divers have Mark's knowledge of the underwater terrain off southern California and I am indebted to him for his assistance and patience. Mark was another of my reviewers whose help I could not have done without.

Juan Salvador probably spends more time in the water hunting than any other diver in Santa Barbara. A proficient free diver *and* scuba diver, he also has an outgoing personality. Many thanks to Johnny for sharing numerous stories of his underwater adventures.

Former Navy diver Mike Ward has been an avid underwater hunter on Florida's gulf coast for many years. His insights on the tropical species covered in the book are the result of many hours underwater.

A special acknowledgment goes to Brian Bradley, owner of the Blue Water Hunter dive store in Goleta, California. Brian opened his store to me and gave me access to his equipment for photographic purposes. He also provided me with extensive information.

Numerous equipment manufacturers provided equipment for me to use and photograph in the production of this book. Ed O'Keefe of Mares provided their excellent Cyrano pneumatic gun and accessories. Ute Packi of JBL Enterprises made sure I had several models of their popular pole spears, guns, and tips when I needed them. Ray Bullion of Sea Bear helped me secure their superb Russian pneumatic spearguns. Peter Riedell of Spears by Riedell shared technical information and was always willing to provide me with quality equipment.

Carole Branco of Long Beach Island Scuba shared information on east coast spearfishing techniques and targets. Tommy Durrance of Florida also shared his knowledge of the specific equipment and techniques used in the warm waters found there.

Carol Rose of the Underwater Society of America helped with information on competitive spearfishing.

Bill Gleason at *Skin Diver Magazine* graciously gave me permission to use an old cover of *Skin Diver* and several ads. *Skin Diver* is the oldest continuous sport diving publication in the United States.

Professional underwater photographers Jesse Cancelmo and Bob Evans each provided great photos for the book. Jesse has been published in numerous diving magazines and is a top notch underwater photographer. Bob's photos have been published in books and magazines around the world. Pete Ryan, Nick Stobaugh, and Jim Finch also contributed some great photos.

My publisher, Jim Joiner, enthusiastically supported this project from its inception. His patience, assistance, and friendship are always appreciated.

As usual, my wife Kristine Barsky is the catalyst that makes my work come to life. Nobody is as patient as Kristine, whether she is reviewing text, modeling for underwater photos, shooting photos, or helping me clean our boat after a long day of diving. Although she is a full time professional marine biologist, she understands and values the achievements of the underwater hunters who are our friends. Without Kristine, my best projects would only be mediocre. I could never ask for a better wife.

Steven M. Barsky

INTRODUCTION

This book is intended for the novice skin or scuba diver who wants to get started in spearfishing. Whether you choose to hunt with scuba or while holding your breath, spearfishing is an exciting and rewarding underwater sport.

There are many people who will tell you that hunting underwater using scuba is "unsportsmanlike". I don't believe this is true. Underwater hunting while free diving is definitely more physically challenging than hunting on scuba, but whether you are a sportsman or not is an entirely different question.

Webster's New World Dictionary defines a sportsman as someone who "takes part in hunting, fishing, etc." Certainly anyone who enjoys spearfishing falls under this definition. The second definition given by Webster's says that a sportsman is someone who, "can take loss or defeat without complaint, or victory without gloating, and who treats his opponents with fairness, generosity, courtesy, etc."

Many dedicated free divers will tell you that it is unfair to hunt underwater while using scuba. Nothing could be further from the truth. Whether you are sportsmanlike or not depends entirely upon your attitude. If you slaughter every fish you see, whether you use scuba or free dive, you are not a sportsman. Similarly, I know many divers, including myself, who have spent hundreds of hours looking for a big halibut without ever firing their gun.

Spearfishing, no matter what gear you use, is a challenging sport. It requires both skill and knowledge. You must develop the skill to take a fish with a single shot, without loss, and minimal suffering to the animal. You must learn the characteristics and habits of the fish you hunt if you want to be successful. Any time you can go into an alien environment and hunt an animal on its own terms, you should feel good about your accomplishment.

In this age of declining fish stocks, you must hunt with a conservation minded attitude. As any biologist will tell you, fishing is an important management tool. As underwater hunters, we can be the most selective fisherman, only taking the exact fish we want and taking no more than we need for our personal consumption.

I hope that you will practice safe spearfishing habits and keep the conservation of our ocean resources always in mind.

Steven M. Barsky

CHAPTER 1

SPEARFISHING IN PERSPECTIVE

Spearfishing was one of the first sport diving activities in this century, but people have certainly speared fish purely for food for as long as men have gone underwater. Many of the world's modern "diving heroes" got started underwater by participating in spearfishing, among other activities. Even underwater naturalists, such as Jacques Cousteau, participated in spearfishing during the birth of modern sport diving.

A BRIEF HISTORY OF SPEARFISHING

Men and women have gone underwater for centuries, for many reasons. Perhaps the original reason to dive beneath the sea was to retrieve an object that was dropped over the side of a boat or pier. However, another early reason to explore the ocean was as simple as the need for food. When people had to feed themselves or starve, and the ocean was close by, some people turned to the sea to gather food to sustain themselves and their families.

One of the earliest records of divers hunting underwater comes from the history of the Bahamas, where the original natives, the Lucayans, were known to engage in spearfishing as early as 1509. There are also records from early Polynesia of natives making goggles from thin pieces of tortoise shells. However, it wasn't until the 1900s when sporting activities became available to the common man, that spearfishing emerged as a popular activity.

In 1929, Guy Gilpatrick, an American living in the south of France, began spearfishing with a small group of friends, as a hobby to amuse himself. He wrote articles about his adventures for the *Saturday Evening Post*, creating interest in the sport among swimmers and other watersports enthusiasts. At that time, there were no fins, masks, snorkels, or spearguns available and Gilpatrick built or improvised his own equipment. He used swimming goggles and hand spears with no power other than his own arm to stab them into the fish.

Gilpatrick may not have been the first underwater sportsman, but he was the first that we know of to write about his diving. In 1938 he published a book entitled *The Compleat Goggler*, the first book on spearfishing.

Spearfishing helped generate an interest in sport diving in the fifties and sixties in the U.S. These early diving books were extremely popular. (Books courtesy of the library of Leslie Leaney.)

In 1933 the first dive club in the United States was formed in San Diego, California. Underwater hunting was the reason for the club's existence. The original founder was Glenn Orr, but the two men who had the biggest impact on modern spearfishing were Wally Potts and Jack Prodanovich.

Potts and Prodanovich created the original rubber powered spearguns in the U.S. All of the modern band guns available today are based on their original designs that were sold to Voit Swimaster and Scubapro. For an excellent history of these early days of spearfishing in the U.S., see Eric Hanauer's book, *Diving Pioneers*, published by Watersport Publishing, Inc.

In 1951, *Skin Diver* magazine first appeared on newsstands in the U.S., originally titled *The Skin Diver*. The magazine was heavily

Skin Diver Magazine was the first regular monthly publication to provide information on spearfishing techniques and equipment.

(Courtesy Skin Diver Magazine.)

oriented towards spearfishing and provided the first monthly communication on developments in the sport. It also carried advertising, providing information on what products were available and where they could be bought.

During the 1950s both pneumatic and spring powered spear guns became readily available. Although spring powered guns are no longer available, pneumatic guns are still quite popular.

Another older speargun design was the CO_2 powered gun. These guns were somewhat similar to the pneumatic guns used today in that both depended on gas pressure to fire the spear, although their operation was different. Some CO_2 guns used a refillable cylinder while others used single CO_2 cartridges. Unlike a pneumatic gun, when a CO_2 gun was fired it released a large cloud of gas bubbles, which some divers felt would scare off a fish.

Probably the last true innovation in spear guns was the "SMG", or Sub Marine Gun, manufactured by the Tapmatic Corp. during a short period in the late 1960s. It was a short, but powerful speargun, with the shaft propelled by

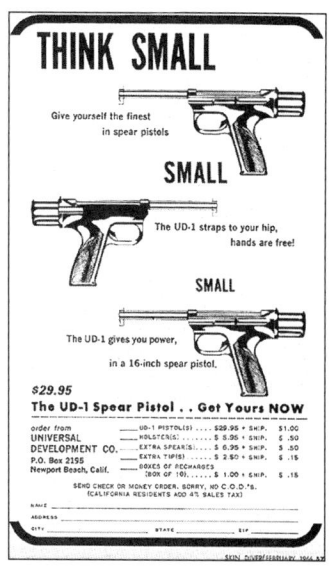

No longer in production, this spear pistol was powered by a CO_2 cartridge.

(Courtesy Skin Diver Magazine.)

Spearfishing in Perspective

.22 caliber cartridges, similar to those used in stud guns and other tools.

The SMG was easy to load and extremely accurate. The gun was available in single, double, and four barrel models. For some reason the gun never caught on and the manufacturer stopped producing it. This was truly a shame because the gun made spearfishing possible for people who didn't have the arm strength or body size required to load larger, more powerful spearguns.

Spearfishing went through a period, from the late seventies through the early nineties, where it was considered "politically incorrect" to participate in the sport. It has only been in the last few years that spearfishing has become acceptable again.

The SMG speargun was powered by .22 caliber cartridges.
(Courtesy Skin Diver Magazine.)

WHY SPEARFISHING?

There are many reasons to participate in spearfishing, some of which are personal, others that seem to satisfy some needs that are felt by many divers. Among the reasons that divers enjoy spearfishing are because they like to eat fresh fish, because they find it challenging, because they enjoy the thrill of the hunt, and because they practice conservation. For many divers the physical activity and exercise benefits are also important, while for others it is the opportunity to select the exact fish that they want.

Perhaps the most common reason for participating in spearfishing is because you enjoy eating freshly caught fish. The difference in taste between what you have taken from the sea only minutes before and the fish you buy in the supermarket is tremendous.

Some of the fish that is sold in markets may be many days or even weeks old. As long as it has not been frozen, the grocer can label it as "fresh". Unless you have a trained eye and can tell the difference between fish that has been recently landed and fish that has been on ice for several weeks, you may be buying seafood that is poor quality. However, almost anyone can _taste_ the difference between freshly caught and "aged" fish, and that difference can be dramatic.

Of course, your nose can also usually tell the difference between a fresh fish and one that should have been used for fertilizer! Even the texture of a fresh fish is much more pleasing than one that has been kept on ice for too long. Once you start spearfishing, you'll become much more discriminating about the fish you eat!

There is nothing better than a meal of freshly caught fish.

Imagine yourself on a beach at sunset, after a day of diving with friends. As the sun goes down, the coals from a driftwood fire are glowing red hot. Corn and baked potatoes are cooking over the fire, you can smell the garlic from hot bread, and a big, cold, green salad is waiting. You finish filleting your freshly caught fish, sprinkle it with lemon juice, herbs, and spices, and place it over the fire. In minutes, it's done as everyone crowds around to enjoy the meal. What could be more fun than this?

Part of what makes a fresh fish meal so rewarding is the effort and energy that had to be expended to get it. Making a perfect shot on a large fish and landing it without a struggle is every bit as challenging as taking a great underwater photograph. Spearfishing demands that the diver have skill, determination, and endurance. Of course, there are always the great stories to tell about how you landed the fish that will make your meal more memorable.

Many divers find that they take as much enjoyment from the "thrill of the hunt" as they do in actually landing their catch. To be a successful spearfisherman you must develop effective stalking techniques that allow you to get close to fish without spooking them. This can be more difficult to do on scuba than while free diving, although I know underwater hunters who have landed white seabass and yellowtail while using compressed air.

In today's environmentally conscious world, most people would probably be confused if you tried to explain to them that by participating in spearfishing you could actually be aiding conservation, but it's true. Many people find this concept difficult to understand.

As a spearfisherman, when you select a large fish as your target and selectively remove it from the population of fish in a particular area, you are making room for a juvenile fish to grow, mature, and reproduce. The older, larger fish may be past its prime sexual reproductive capacity, but by its very presence it may be occupying a niche that younger fish cannot challenge.

In most cases in nature, animals of the same species are the biggest competition for food and mating in the survival of the fittest. As a selective hunter, you can contribute to this natural cycle of life. Most state fishing regulations are designed to encourage this type of resource development.

SPEARFISHING IN THE AGE OF CONSERVATION

It is not uncommon today to meet people who are opposed to the killing of any animal. They believe that all life is sacred and that no animal should be killed for any reason, particularly where animals are hunted for sport. They have strong moral beliefs that should be respected.

It is clear that spearfishermen, or anyone who eats any type of animal, will never be able to reach an agreement on the morality of hunting with those who are opposed to all killing of animals. Yet, it is essential for all spearfishermen to practice underwater hunting in a manner that is ethical and has the utmost consideration for the lives of the fish that are taken in our sport. In this regards, underwater hunters would do well to look to the native American Indians as role models for the proper attitude that the modern day spearfisherman should adopt.

When the Indians roamed the plains, hunting buffalo, they approached the killing of these animals as a sacred religious act. They believed they took on the spirit of these animals when they ate them and every kill was marked with respect.

You don't have to be religious to appreciate how tough it is for any animal to survive and grow to maturity in the sea. When you kill a fish underwater, you should show respect for the animal whose life you have taken. In many cases, fish are long lived animals, with some larger fish having lives equal in length to man's. Survival in the ocean is not easy and for every fish that has grown to a respectable size, hundreds, if not thousands, of its brothers and sisters have perished from one cause or another.

To help ensure that there will be large fish for you to hunt tomorrow, and in the distant future, it is essential to follow a few simple rules of conservation. These rules generally go beyond whatever fishing regulations may be in effect locally, but make sense based upon what we know about marine life today.

- Only spear a fish when you know exactly what species it is, as well as the legal size, and open season for taking it. Size limits and seasons are usually based upon the reproductive traits of these creatures. By taking an undersize or immature animal you have eliminated that fish's chances to reproduce, decreasing your chances of taking fish next year or the year after.

- Only spear a fish when you have a good shot and know that you can reasonably land that fish. A "gut shot", where you hit the fish in the stomach, will usually lead you to lose the fish. Most fish wounded in this way will not survive, either due to predators who sense their injury, or infection, which causes the fish to weaken and die.

- Take only as much fish as your immediate family can consume when it is fresh. Don't try to feed your entire neighborhood and all of your family's relatives. Only take fish that you intend to eat.

Divers who don't follow local fishing laws or who fail to hunt with a positive attitude towards conservation, place the sport of spearfishing at risk for everyone. There are numerous animal rights activists, as well as conservationists, who keep a watchful eye on the ocean. When you show up on the beach with a bag limit that exceeds what conservation dictates you provide ammunition for anyone who would like to see spearfishing made illegal. In today's world, the spearfisherman is competing with both commercial as well recreational fishermen for the same resource.

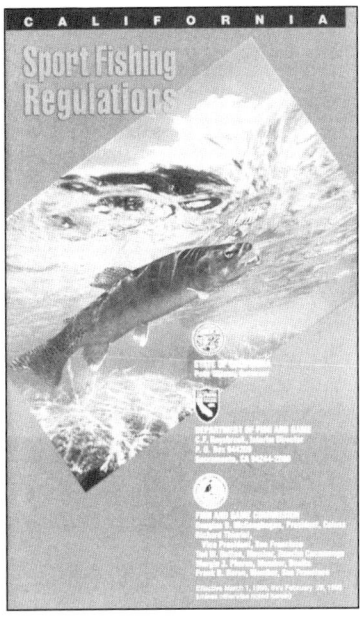

Please be sure to follow all local fishing laws as well as the ethical standards of conservation.

It is all too easy for these other groups to point towards divers as "unfair competitors" for species of fish that they choose to target. There are more and more people looking to utilize our dwindling resources. There is also increased pressure on fish stocks due to loss of habitat as coastal areas are developed and pollution occurs.

Please do your part to make sure that spearfishing maintains a positive image in the public eye. A good spearfisherman is not embarrassed to come home empty handed, but is ashamed to come home with a fish that is small or inedible.

As a concerned diver, you are in the best position to see what is happening to our underwater resources. If you can see that a particular species is becoming rare in your area, or if you know that stocks of a particular fish are dwindling, the proper ethical and moral decision would be to refrain from hunting that species until the stocks have had a chance to restore themselves. With today's technology, such as GPS, chart plotters, and fish finders, it is almost too easy to return to the smallest reef, placing extreme pressure on what might otherwise be an isolated population of animals. Develop a conservation ethic and there will be fish to hunt next year and for your children's children.

A large fish is usually quite old. These two halibut could be as old as 30 years of age.

NOTES

CHAPTER 2

TYPES OF SPEARFISHING GEAR

There are many different types of spearguns and equipment available today, and it's not unusual to hear avid spearfishermen argue the merits of different types of guns. Like most dive equipment, however, a particular gun is usually only good for a particular purpose and there is no one best speargun. In fact, it is not unusual for a serious spearfisherman to own several styles of guns that are used to hunt either particular species of fish, or used in specific types of underwater habitats.

The main types of gear most commonly seen today include the polespear, the band powered gun, and the pneumatic gun. Of course, there are variations on these designs, but these are the general categories.

HAWAIIAN SLINGS

A Hawaiian sling is not a polespear, although many divers who have heard of this equipment think they are one and the same. It would be difficult to find a true Hawaiian sling for sale in most dive stores in the U.S. today.

The Hawaiian sling lies somewhere between a true polespear and a speargun. Whether it was truly developed in Hawaii or elsewhere in Polynesia is unknown, but at one time it was a popular type of spearfishing equipment. Hawaiian slings are rarely seen today.

The true Hawaiian sling consists of a steel spear shaft with a tip and a piece of hard tubing that will accommodate the blunt end of the spear. This "guide tube" serves as a barrel to aim the spear. A piece of rubber surgical tubing is attached on two opposite sides of the opening on the same end of the tube. A metal cap is fitted in the far end of the loop of surgical tubing.

To use the Hawaiian sling, you insert the shaft through the hard tube, holding the tube with one hand, out in front of your body with your elbow locked. With your other hand, you place the blunt end of the shaft in the cap at the end of the surgical tubing and pull back on the shaft and surgical tubing at the same time, much as you would a bow and arrow.

The distance the shaft will travel is determined by the amount of strength you have to pull the surgical tubing back towards you. However, your maximum pull is limited by the length of your arms.

You aim the shaft by moving your arm that holds the tube up, down, or side to side, towards your target. Your aim is also influenced by the movement of the arm stretching the surgical tubing.

To use a Hawaiian sling, with power and accuracy, requires a great deal of skill, more than that required to use either a polespear or a speargun. Although most fish taken with this type of gear today are probably relatively small, under 25 pounds, a talented Hawaiian sling user can land fish that are much larger. It is also a simple piece of gear, with little maintenance required other than to replace the bands on an occasional basis and rinse it with fresh water after use.

One of the limitations of the Hawaiian sling is that once the spear is fired, if you don't get an immediate kill, the fish is free to swim off with

This Seabear polespear is very similar to the original Hawaiian sling design.

your spear. The shaft is not fastened to the tube in any way. If you don't have another shaft immediately available to finish the fish off you may lose your first spear. Using this type of gear in areas of poor visibility is impractical at best.

POLESPEARS

A polespear is the simplest piece of spearfishing gear available today and still one of the best. Polespears are economical, easy to use, simple to maintain, and much safer to use than any type of speargun.

Most polespears today are made from either fiberglass or aluminum. Fiberglass models are generally solid all the way through the shaft, while aluminum models are usually made from aluminum tubing. Fiberglass polespears are heavier by their design than aluminum polespears, although most aluminum models are designed to be filled with water to give them increased weight and hitting power. Others, such as those manufactured by Spears by Riedel, Inc. have sufficient weight to make them negatively buoyant without the need to fill the shaft with water.

Hitting or stopping power is an important consideration, whether you use a polespear or a speargun. The heavier the weight of the shaft, the more penetration you will get, provided you have sufficient power to move the shaft through the water at reasonable speed. Penetration is essential to damage the fish's spine or brain and stop it from swimming away. The impact of the shaft also provides a certain amount of damage and shock to the fish, that will also help to stop it from moving.

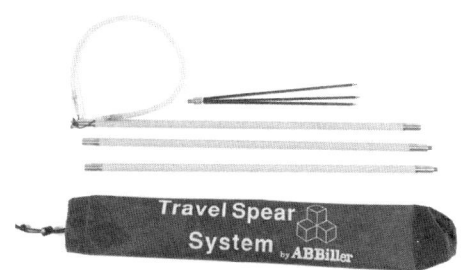

This AB Biller polespear is made from aluminum and disassembles for travel.

Both fiberglass and aluminum spears generally are available as single length spears or as "take-down" models. Take-down polespears can be disassembled for travel or assembled at the size you choose according to conditions. Take-down polespears provide the most convenience and flexibility in their application.

Polespears come in a variety of lengths, although most are between five and seven feet in length. Longer spears are generally

Place your open hand in the loop so that the rubber lays between your thumb and index finger and stretch the band.

heavier and have more hitting power. They also can potentially have more power if you have the strength to stretch the surgical tubing further along the shaft. However, longer spears are not as maneuverable, particularly around rocks and thick kelp.

When selecting a polespear, be sure to see what size spear feels comfortable for you to handle. Evaluate both the length of the spear, the diameter, and the weight of the shaft. If you normally wear gloves while diving it is important to see how the spear feels in your gloved hand. If you can, rent or borrow several different models before making your purchase.

Some polespears come with fixed heads that cannot be changed, while others can be fitted with any head you choose. The most popular spearhead used with polespears is the paralyzer tip, which is a three pronged head that helps to immobilize the fish if you have adequate penetration. As the tip enters the fish it tends to spread, helping to prevent movement of the fish.

To use a polespear, you hold the spear with one hand and place the open loop of surgical tubing in the palm of your other hand. Stretch the tubing by pulling towards the tip of the spear with the tubing held in the gap between your thumb and forefinger. When you have stretched the tubing as far as possible, grab the spear with the same hand that you are using to stretch the loop of surgical tubing. Hold the spear and the loop of tubing tightly, so your hand doesn't slip on the shaft. Remove your other hand from the polespear.

When you see a fish you want to shoot, and you are sufficiently close to it, open your hand and the polespear will leap forward. However, you must keep your hand in the loop of surgical tubing or you will lose the spear if your first shot isn't a kill shot.

Like the Hawaiian sling, the big advantage to the pole spear is its simplicity and ease of maintenance. Polespears are also safer than spearguns and relatively inexpensive when compared to spearguns.

Polespears are not usually used for fish in excess of 15-20 pounds, although there are many west coast divers who have taken large halibut using polespears. The major disadvantage to the polespear is its relatively short range when compared to a speargun. Like the Hawaiian sling, the effective range of the polespear is limited by your own strength and the length of the spear.

Polespears are a good way to gain your initial experience in spearfishing. If you become proficient in the use of a polespear, your accuracy with a speargun will generally be excellent.

To maintain your polespear, just be sure to give it a thorough rinse at the end of the day. Sharpen the tip occasionally using a file or stone. Inspect the rubber sling periodically and replace it when it shows signs of wear or rot. A good quality pole spear should last you forever.

Even if you normally leave your collapsible pole spear assembled, it should be disassembled for cleaning after use in salt water. After rinsing, spray the threads with a small amount of WD-40® or other corrosion inhibitor. Shown here is a JBL collapsible polespear.

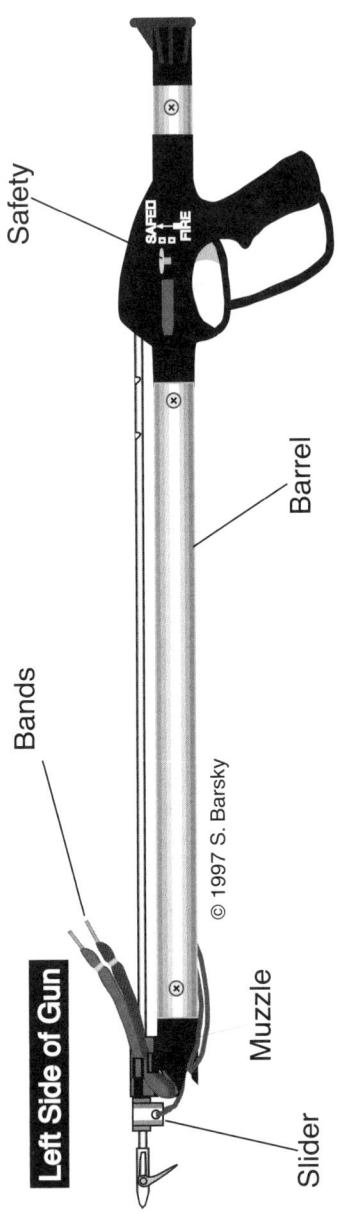

These drawings shows the parts and nomenclature for a "typical" speargun.

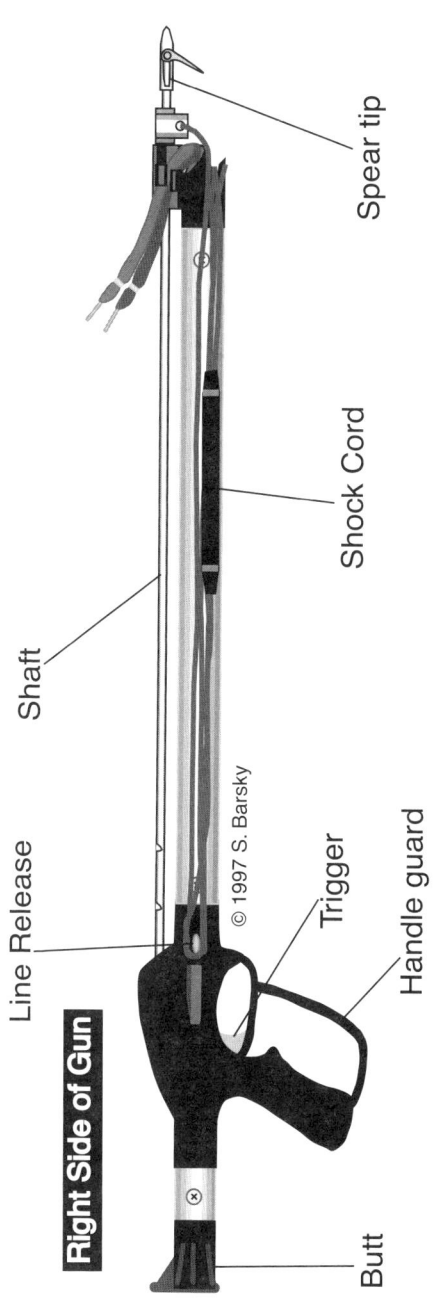

Types of Spearfishing Gear

Current Types of Spearguns

Band Guns

Band guns are probably the most popular type of spearguns available today. Most have simple mechanisms that require only a minimum of maintenance and attention. With proper care, a good quality band gun can last for your entire diving career.

One of the earliest mass produced band guns was the "Arbalete" which was manufactured by Spirotechnique in France. The Arbalete was the name for a particular design and is <u>not</u> the name for all rubber powered guns, although you may hear older divers refer to all band guns as "arbaletes".

Band guns always include a muzzle (or some variation) to hold the bands, a barrel, a trigger mechanism, a line release mechanism, bands made from surgical tubing, a butt, and a shaft. No matter who makes the gun, these basic elements must always be present, although there may be great variety in their design and the materials used for fabrication.

To prevent the spear from being lost, most spearguns use a "slide" or "slider" on the shaft and a length of line which is attached to both the slide and the gun. More expensive guns, such as those manufactured by Riffe, use a shaft with "fins" that project up from the shaft. The fins are used to engage the bands.

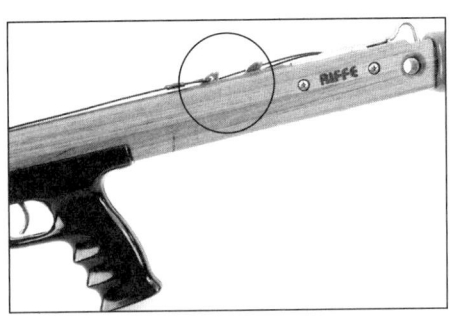

Riffe uses a drilled fin on their shafts as an attachment point for the line.

Spears by Riedel manufactures a wide variety of guns and polespears. Their guns are made from high quality materials.

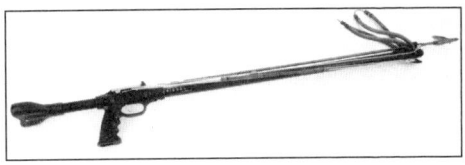

Riffe guns are manufactured by Jay Riffe, a legendary spearfisherman.

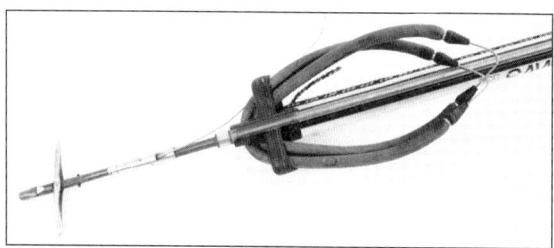

JBL offers their Sawed-off Magnum with an open muzzle.

Instead of using a slide, Riffe drills one of the fins on the shaft and the line is attached to the fin.

The shaft is held in the gun by the muzzle and the trigger mechanism. The band (or bands) mount at the muzzle and are stretched back to a notch (or notches) in the shaft. As mentioned previously, some shafts are not notched but use fins that stick up above the shaft.

Each band is equipped with a metal wishbone, or a piece of string, that hooks into the notch in the shaft and puts the shaft under enormous tension. When the trigger is pulled, the shaft flies forward out of the muzzle of the gun.

Materials used for the fabrication of gun barrels typically include aluminum tubing and wood. Aluminum guns are usually somewhat lighter than wooden guns and less expensive, but aluminum barrels are rugged and will last almost forever with little care.

Wooden guns are usually quieter, and more attractive to some divers, but generally require more care to keep them looking good. Most wooden guns are made from teak and should be oiled periodically if you want to keep them looking good and to prevent damage, although some divers take pride in how worn their guns look.

The trigger mechanism inside most guns is usually made from stainless steel. This material rarely needs attention, other than a good rinse at the end of the day. If all of the components of the handle and firing mechanism are metal, a light coating of WD-40® or other corrosion inhibitor to help prevent surface rust is advisable. *However, if there are **any** plastic parts inside the handle, or the handle itself is plastic, **do not use any type of aerosol spray,** as the aerosol propellant used in these sprays may weaken plastic parts and cause them to fail.*

The muzzle may be made from a variety of materials. The purpose of the muzzle is to provide a place to mount the bands and to align the shaft so that it "flies" straight when it leaves the gun. Some guns, such as the Riffe do not have a conventional muzzle; instead, the bands are held in place in a slot that is part of the barrel. On newer Riffe guns the spear merely lays in a groove in the barrel.

Some divers prefer band guns with an open muzzle. The advantage to this design is that the entire length of the shaft does not need to be threaded through the muzzle, which can be awkward underwater. Instead, the notched end of the shaft can be inserted in the trigger mechanism and the end with the tip can be dropped into the muzzle. This is a much faster way to reload, especially if you miss a shot. Guns without muzzles are also somewhat quieter when fired.

Some band powered spearguns are designed with safety mechanisms while others are not. There are actually several good reasons for <u>not</u> including a safety mechanism in a speargun, but probably the best one is that any time the bands are loaded the gun must be considered armed. Some divers feel that a safety offers a false sense of security. Once a speargun is loaded it must never be pointed at anyone, whether it has its safety engaged or not.

Another reason that some manufacturers do not include

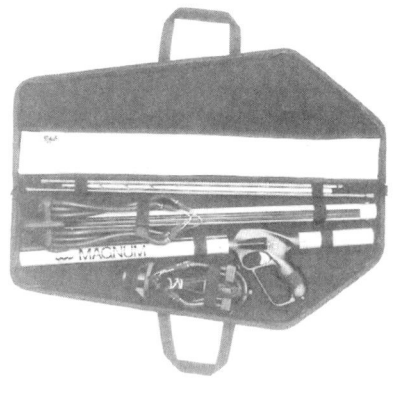

Certain models of JBL guns are designed so that the barrel, shaft, and bands can be changed according to where you are hunting and the local conditions. This can save you money that might otherwise be spent on multiple guns.

safety mechanisms is that they can jam in either position, rendering the gun useless until it is disassembled. In addition, some safety mechanisms are noisy and produce a distinct "click" when released that will scare away fish.

Spearguns are extremely powerful underwater weapons. Numerous divers have been killed or severely injured through the improper handling of spearguns. Spearguns must be treated with the same respect that you would treat a firearm. They are potentially lethal weapons.

Spearguns are particularly dangerous if they are loaded out of the water. Their topside range far exceeds their relatively short range underwater. Never load a speargun out of the water and be sure to unload all spearguns before bringing them back aboard a boat. Some dive boats on the west coast have a policy of taking any speargun that has been brought aboard in a loaded condition and throwing it back over the side of the boat!

Shorter band guns are generally designed for hunting around rocks and reefs, and for shooting smaller fish. Larger band guns are designed for longer range and larger fish.

Some manufacturers, such as JBL, have designed band guns that allow you to change the barrel, the shaft and the bands according to where you plan to hunt on a particular day. For example, if visibility is poor or you will be shooting smaller fish, you can use the shorter barrel, bands, and shaft supplied with the gun. When visibility is better, or if you are working in open water, you can switch to a longer barrel, shaft, and bands. This only works with guns where the barrel can be changed out, which are generally guns with aluminum barrels.

Some band powered guns can also be used with a variety of shaft diameters to give you a choice of how much hitting power you want to use on a given day. Generally speaking, the larger the fish you are hunting, the heavier the shaft (larger diameter) you want to use. Again, this is the equivalent of the difference between hunting with a .22 caliber rifle and a high powered deer rifle.

Beware of using a shaft that is too long with your gun. The more the shaft extends past the end of the muzzle, the lower the gun will shoot, which may cause you to miss or wound a fish. This should be avoided.

Avoid adding too many bands to your gun, even if the shaft is notched for additional bands beyond what is supplied with the gun. When you overpower your gun it will not shoot accurately and the recoil could cause serious injury if the gun strikes your body or head. Similarly, it's wise to avoid using bands that have too much power for your gun. Whenever you replace your bands use the bands sold by the manufacturer for your specific make and model of gun.

One of the potential problems with some band powered speargun designs is that when the shaft is released and moves along the barrel it whips up and down before it leaves the end of the muzzle. This happens so fast that you can't see it, but it definitely creates a sound that fish can hear. Different gun designers have come up with a variety of methods to get around this problem, but the most common is to create a groove in the barrel that serves as a channel for the shaft. Ideally, you want your gun to be as quiet as possible because any sound you make may spook a fish.

Most modern spearguns are designed to float when the shaft is removed and you should definitely check to see that any gun you buy has this feature. In the event that a fish takes off with your gun you have some hope of retrieving it if it floats, and you have enough line for it to be up off the bottom. Conversely, the gun should be either neutral or slightly negative when the shaft is in the gun, so you can set it down on the bottom if you need to adjust your gear and need both hands. Keep in mind, however, that the addition of a reel, line pack, or other accessories will change the buoyancy of the gun, and may cause it to sink even after the shaft has been fired.

Some band powered spearguns have the handle located in the middle of the gun, while other have the handle located at the end. Many divers feel that mid-handle guns are somewhat easier to maneuver underwater since you don't have the entire length of the gun sticking out away from you. However, mid-handle guns generally have less power unless the gun has a push-rod mechanism on the rear of the gun and the bands stretch the entire length of the gun.

To load a band powered gun the first step is to slide the notched end of the shaft through the muzzle (if so equipped) and insert the shaft so that it properly engages the trigger mechanism. If the gun is equipped with a conventional muzzle and slider, it will probably be machined so that the slider will fit into the muzzle and help align the shaft. If there is a safety it must be engaged at this time.

The line is strung from the front of the gun (where the bands are) to the line release mechanism which is normally located near the trigger on the handle. The section of line that includes the elastic shock cord is strung last. This makes it easier to fasten the line on the gun. If the shock cord is the first wrap on the gun you won't be able to take advantage of the stretch of the elastic and the friction of the line will make it difficult to get the last wrap of line on the gun.

If your gun is equipped with a safety be sure to engage it. The safety should be engaged before the gun is cocked.

To load your gun you must first thread the shaft into the muzzle, if it isn't already in position.

If your gun has a conventional muzzle, the slider must engage it properly and the shaft must engage the trigger mechanism.

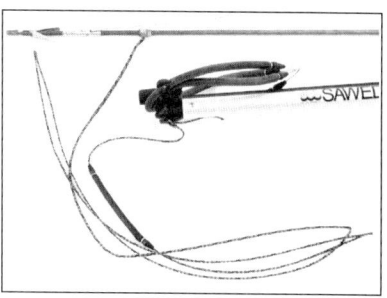

Types of Spearfishing Gear

The line must be strung properly so that it will release immediately when the gun is fired.

Cock the gun by pulling back steadily on the bands with both hands. Stretch the outermost band so it engages the rearmost notch in the shaft. The next band engages the second notch from the rear and so on.

To cock the bands, the butt of the gun is usually placed against either your weight belt buckle or your hip. Some wetsuits designed for free diving have special "cocking pads" located in the center of the chest to make it easier to load the gun. If your gun is equipped with multiple bands you will usually want to grab the bottom band first and pull it toward the rear of the gun in a single, smooth motion.

Some spearshafts are notched to accept metal wishbones, while others, such as Riffe's, have projections on the shaft to accept the nylon line used to string the bands. Whichever design you have on your shaft, the bands must fully engage the shaft. Depending on where and what you are hunting you may not

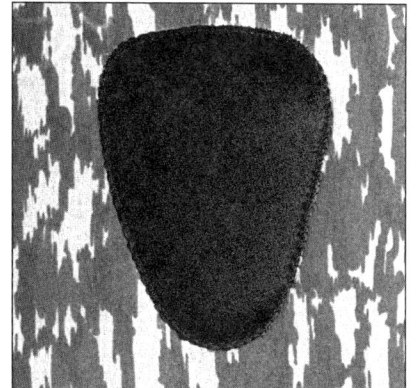

A cocking pad on your wetsuit can help to cushion your chest if you prefer to brace your gun against your sternum while loading it. This design was developed by the Blue Water Hunter dive shop in Goleta, California.

want to load all of the bands, but your gun will only have its maximum power when all bands are cocked.

Once the gun is cocked, carry it by the handle or if you need to support it, place your second hand underneath the barrel. Do not carry it with your hand clutching the bands when they are cocked. If for any reason the bands slip or break you could injure your hand.

Keep in mind that there is always the possibility for the bands to break while they are under tension. It is also possible to have the wishbone, whether string or metal, pull out from the bands or break. If either of these events occurs you can be seriously injured.

Aiming a speargun is not exactly like aiming a handgun or rifle. Where most firearms are aimed by aligning a set of front and rear sights, spearguns are normally fired by what's known as "instinct shooting", where you concentrate on the target and swing your arm and the gun where you want it to aim. Some divers prefer to sight down the shaft feeling this gives them greater accuracy. You will need to experiment to see which method works best for you.

To fire the gun, aim it at your target holding the gun by one hand away from your body and squeeze the trigger. If you have a smaller gun, your free hand should be completely clear of the gun. This free hand is often unconsciously or consciously used to stabilize the diver.

If you have a large gun, you must use two hands to get an accurate shot. In this situation, one hand holds the handle while your other hand holds the butt end of the gun. This helps stabilize the gun, minimizes recoil effects, and helps prevent injury.

Never hold the gun up to your face during firing. This will help to protect you from the recoil of the gun which could knock your mask off your face or cause serious injury.

When you fire your gun the line will automatically release and the bands will spring forward. If you miss your shot, it will generally take you a few minutes to sort out the line and the bands for reloading. In most cases, the bands will be twisted or misaligned and not in the proper position for cocking the gun. Take your time and sort it out properly before attempting to reload your gun.

The major advantages of a speargun over a polespear is that a gun is generally more accurate, has a greater range, and has more hitting and stopping power. To take large fish, it is essential to have a speargun. To shoot fish at longer ranges, over six feet away, you must have a speargun.

Spearguns are generally much more expensive than polespears. In almost all cases, the larger the gun, the more expensive it is. Another disadvantage to spearguns is that they are more difficult to load than polespears. The larger the gun, the more difficult it is to load.

When you select a speargun you must consider where you hunt, the species you want to hunt, and how big a gun you can load. Evaluate

Be sure to rinse your gun thoroughly with fresh water after using it.

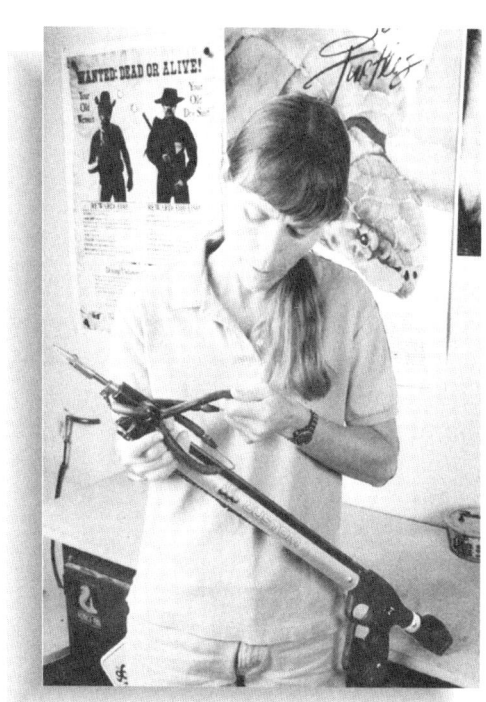

Inspect the bands of your gun before you leave for a dive trip to be sure they are in good condition. Worn bands can break easily and may cause personal injury.

how the grip feels in your hand while wearing gloves, the trigger action, the line release mechanism, and the ruggedness of the gun. Again, see if you can rent or borrow the model gun you are considering for purchase.

Just because you can load a large, powerful speargun doesn't mean that you should always carry a large gun. There will be days when the visibility is poor and it isn't safe to use a large gun, or you are hunting smaller fish that would be destroyed by a larger gun. Choose your gun according to the visibility, your location, and your intended target.

Spearguns require more maintenance than polespears. Be sure to give your gun a thorough rinse after each day of diving. Inspect the bands and replace them when they begin to crack or look gummy. Depending on the design of your gun, you may want to give the mechanism a light coat of silicone grease or similar lubrication to keep the mechanism operating smoothly. Avoid using silicone spray or any aerosol spray near plastic parts.

Matt Lum built this custom gun for taking larger fish like these white seabass.

Custom Guns

Most custom guns are large, overgrown, band powered spearguns that are normally made by an individual underwater hunter for a specific purpose. Most serious spearfishermen and especially competitive spearfishermen eventually decide to build their own guns. There is something very satisfying about sitting down with a knife and building your own gun that you then use to get your own food.

Custom guns are usually made from a hard wood that will hold up well in the marine environment and the most common material used is teak. While some builders will design their own trigger mechanisms, many of them will use off-the-shelf rigs from manufacturers such as Riffe or Alexander.

Many of the divers who build their own guns get quite elaborate in their decoration of the gun. Some will inlay pieces of abalone shell or bone. Others will burn drawings into the gun or even name the gun.

Custom guns are normally used for hunting large, powerful fish, such as giant sea bass or white seabass, or yellowtail. They aren't designed for hunting on a shallow reef for 15 pound fish.

Custom guns are normally rigged with special line packs, floats, or other buoys. These accessories will be discussed in Chapter #3.

Seabear's pneumatic guns are very powerful and accurate. They come in a variety of sizes, as do most pneumatic guns.

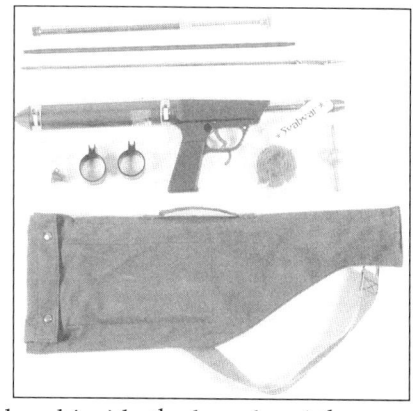

Pneumatic Guns

Pneumatic guns are spearguns that use compressed air to power an internal piston that propels the shaft. When the shaft is placed inside the barrel and the gun is loaded, the piston is compressed. When you pull the trigger, the piston springs forward, ejecting the spear.

Pneumatic guns tend to be more popular in Europe than they are in the United States. Mares in Italy makes a very popular pneumatic gun and Sea Bear imports a well made pneumatic gun from Russia.

Pneumatic guns use more complicated mechanisms than band powered spear guns. The internal tolerances in pneumatic guns must be more precise to keep the pressure inside the gun from leaking out. These guns have o-ring seals and the internal mechanism is filled with oil to provide lubrication for the moving parts and o-ring seals. The barrels inside pneumatic guns must be machined to close tolerances so that the spear does not wobble inside the barrel as it is fired.

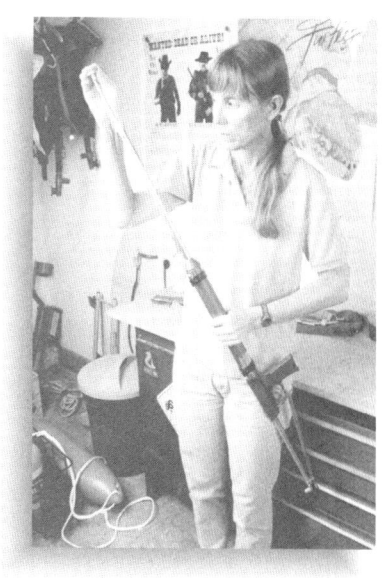

Never pressurize a pneumatic gun beyond the manufacturer's recommendations. Overpressurization could cause the seals to fail or the barrel to explode.

Be sure to activate the safety on the gun.

To load a pneumatic gun you will need to brace the handle against the top of your thigh or foot.

It is essential to keep sand or other foreign matter out of the barrel of your pneumatic gun. If sand is allowed to enter the barrel it can score it and cause the mechanism to lose pressure.

Pneumatic guns are among the most powerful guns for their size relative to band powered guns. Even a very compact pneumatic gun has lots of power. Like band powered guns, pneumatic guns are lethal weapons.

Unlike band powered guns, it is not possible to switch to a heavier shaft as conditions change, when using a pneumatic gun. Whatever size shaft is supplied with the gun when you buy it is the one you must use.

Some people contend that pneumatic guns are more accurate than band powered guns. While logically this would seem to be true, since spears from pneumatic guns are propelled in a similar fashion to a cartridge from a firearm, there have been no published scientific tests to support this claim. In all probability, the skill of the hunter outweighs any differences in accuracy between guns.

Make sure the line is strung so it will release when the gun is fired.

Take care not to lose the loader for your gun. You can attach a clip to the loader and hang it from your buoyancy compensator. On Mares' guns the loader can be stored in a cavity in the base of the handle.

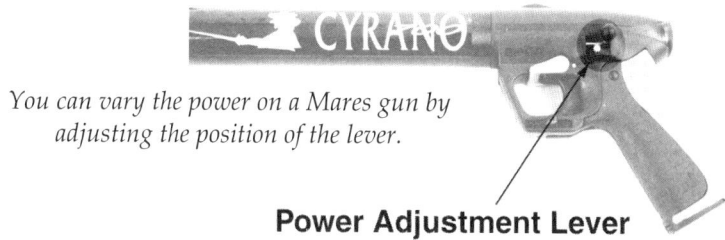

You can vary the power on a Mares gun by adjusting the position of the lever.

Power Adjustment Lever

    Pneumatic guns must be pressurized to the correct pressure in order to keep them working properly. All pneumatic gun manufacturers supply their guns with a pump that is used specifically for this purpose. The pump will normally thread into the end of the barrel and is operated by hand. See the owner's manual supplied with your gun for specific pumping instructions.

Never pressurize your pneumatic gun beyond the maximum pressure recommended by the manufacturer. If the gun is over-pressurized the barrel can fail and cause severe personal injury.

Not all pneumatic guns float when the shaft is removed so be sure to consult your owner's manual in regards to the particular characteristics of your gun. Remember that if you add accessories, their buoyancy will affect the buoyancy of the gun.

To load a pneumatic gun, you must use the "loader" that is supplied with the gun. Before you begin to load the gun be sure that the safety is armed so that the gun will not fire accidentally. The handle of the gun is placed so that the back side of the handle rests on your thigh or the top of your foot. The spear is placed in the barrel and the loader is used to cushion your hand as you push the shaft down inside the barrel. Force the shaft down the barrel until the shaft clicks into position. If you lose your grip with the loader as you compress the piston the shaft will fly out of the gun and could injure you. Make sure you are not looking down at the spear as you load your gun – keep your head away from any possible contact with the tip or shaft.

Although pneumatic guns load differently than band powered guns, it still takes considerable effort to load a large pneumatic gun. Be sure that you can load any gun you select before you make your final purchase. Does the gun appear rugged enough to withstand the abuse it will receive while diving? Are the controls easy to operate, particularly if the water in your area is cold and you must wear gloves to protect your hands?

On some guns, such as the Mares, you can vary the power of the gun from shot to shot by activating a lever on the side of the handle mechanism. This is a nice feature that allows you to set the gun according to where and what you are hunting on any given day.

The advantages of pneumatic guns include their high power/length ratio and their accuracy. One of the disadvantages is their cost, which tends to be a bit higher than band powered guns. Their internal complexity also means that in most cases, the guns must be returned to the manufacturer for repairs.

Maintenance of pneumatic guns includes a thorough rinsing of the gun at the end of a day of use. In addition, depending upon the type of gun you own, the gun may need to be stored with the barrel either up or down. Consult your owner's manual for the proper method of storage for your gun.

If your gun will not hold pressure or leaks excessive amounts of oil, it means that the internal seals are worn. In this situation the gun must be returned to the dealer or manufacturer. Never attempt to service a pneumatic gun by yourself. If the gun is serviced improperly it may not work correctly and this could lead to accidents.

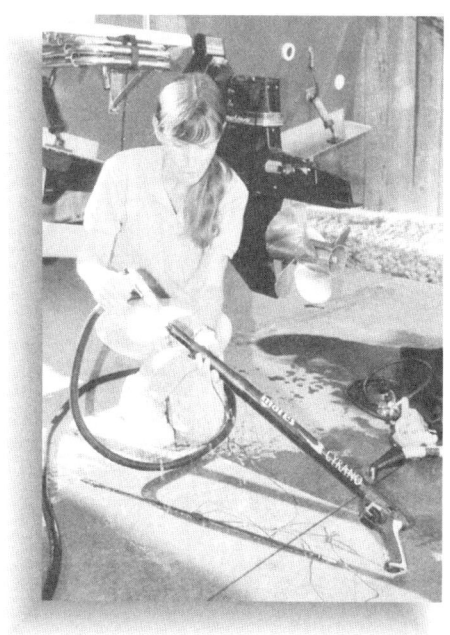

Always rinse your pneumatic gun carefully after a day of diving.

NOTES

CHAPTER 3

SPEARFISHING ACCESSORIES

In spearfishing, like most sports, after you have purchased the basic speargun, there are still some accessories you will need in order to fully enjoy a day in the water.

SPEAR TIPS FOR POLESPEARS

As mentioned previously, some polespears have threaded ends so that you can use many of the same spear tips that are used with spearguns. Popular tips for use with polespears include single barb heads, gig heads, and paralyzers.

The simplest type of spear tip is the single barb head. This is the type of tip that is supplied with most smaller guns and is designed for hunting smaller fish. It has limited holding power and should not be used on fish much in excess of five pounds, or

Single barb tips are designed to be used only on small fish.

any fish that has soft flesh.

Another tip that is popular for smaller fish is the gig style head with multiple barbs, typically either a trident (three barb) or a four barb head. These heads have more shocking power in that they create multiple wounds, but they do not have a great deal of penetrating ability. This type of head is more commonly seen on smaller spearguns.

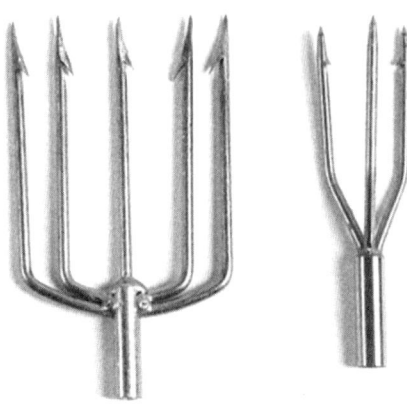

Gig heads have shocking power, but are not good for complete penetration.

Paralyzer heads are probably the most popular design for use with polespears today. They offer both good penetration, holding and stopping power.

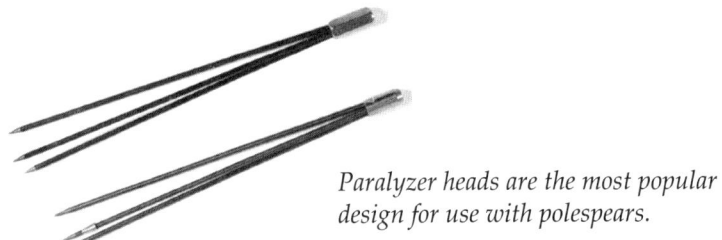

Paralyzer heads are the most popular design for use with polespears.

SPEAR TIPS FOR SPEARGUNS

Although spear tips are classified here as accessory items, you must have a spear tip to hunt successfully. However, since spear tips are removable, and there are so many choices available, you can't truly consider a spear tip as part of the gun. Most divers own several tips that are changed according to the target for the day.

Twin barb spear tips are designed for use on larger, more powerful fish that weigh over eight pounds, but not for fish with soft flesh. The twin barb head has more holding power, and the barbs are normally set to spread once the head enters the fish. Some twin barb heads are designed to spin, so that the fish cannot spin the head off the shaft. However, it's a good idea to use some

Loctite® 222 Small Screw Threadlocker on the threads of the shaft to help prevent this from happening.

On most twin or multi-barb heads designed for larger fish there is a ring that holds the barbs in position to help you pull the head back through the fish. The ring is usually "spring-loaded" through the use of a small piece of rubber installed in the head.

Some divers make the mistake of fastening the barbs under the ring before they fire their gun. In theory, once the head enters the fish, the barbs will open up. This is "theoretical" because many spearfishermen have lost fish when the barbs failed to open. The ring is also supposed to help remove the spear head from the fish by allowing you to capture the barbs so the head can be pulled backwards through the fish.

To avoid any potential ring failure, some divers cut the rings off their spearheads. When they get a fish, they either pinch the barbs together as they feed the shaft back through the fish, or they turn the shaft around to feed it back through so the barbs are naturally forced against the body of the head. Another modification that some divers make is to use large, stainless steel releasable snap swivels on their line so they can detach the shaft from the line and pull only the line and swivel through the fish. If this method is used the pin on the swivel must be closed before you attempt to pull the line through the fish.

If your spearhead is equipped with a ring, and you want to use it, never store it with the barbs under the ring. This can permanently compress the rubber, making the ring useless for its intended purpose until you replace the rubber.

There are many different types of detachable spearheads. The most common type of detachable is designed with twin barbs and a stainless leader between the section that mounts on the shaft and the sharpened tip and barbs. The detachable section

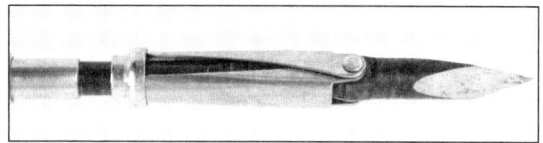

Twin barb heads have great holding power. They should be closed, as seen here, for pulling a shaft back through a fish.

has an o-ring on its base to provide friction and prevent the tip from falling off if your gun is pointed down before you fire it. This type of head requires a definite pull before the head will separate from its base. The design of this head is intended to prevent a fish from gaining leverage against a rock or cave and bending your shaft.

Some divers prefer a detachable head that uses nylon or monofilament to connect the tip to the base of the head. Their rationale is that stainless wire can cut through a fish with soft flesh and that you could lose the fish

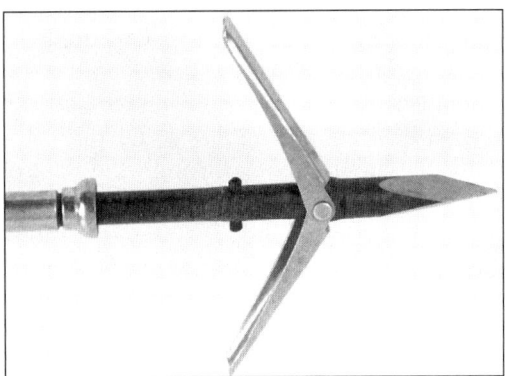

This twin barb head is in the open position.

The slip tip is the other popular detachable head. They are the most streamlined heads, designed for maximum penetration with minimal damage to flesh. Slip tips make a very small hole on entry and exit, unlike heads with larger barbs. The barbs on most slip tips are very tiny and the head is designed to hold in fish that have soft flesh, such as a white seabass.

Unlike detachables with longer barbs and an o-ring on the base of detachable section, slip tips will separate from their base if your gun is tilted downward. To prevent this from happening, some spearfishermen will cut an "o-ring" from a section of surgical tubing and slide it over the slip tip, past the detachable section. The ring is used to hold the detachable portion in place by compressing the cable that secures the head between itself and the base of the head.

Better quality heads use stainless components with stainless wires for detachable heads. The head must be sharp enough to penetrate the skin and scales of the fish you plan to hunt. If you occasionally shoot rocks instead of fish, be sure to carry a file and sharpening stone in your dive bag to sharpen your spearheads when you are ready to shoot fish again. You may also want to carry some spares.

Some manufacturers sell heads that are designated as "rock points" and these are designed for use around rock reefs. Rocks tend to be very hard on spear tips and most people prefer to stop shooting them after a few dives. Of course, some people never tire of shooting rocks while others find that rocks are all that they can hit!

There are literally hundreds of different head designs and each diver generally has his favorites. Talk to other divers in your area and see what they are using before you make your selection.

Always keep your spear tips covered with a cork or plastic sheath. Spear tips are extremely sharp and can cut both you and

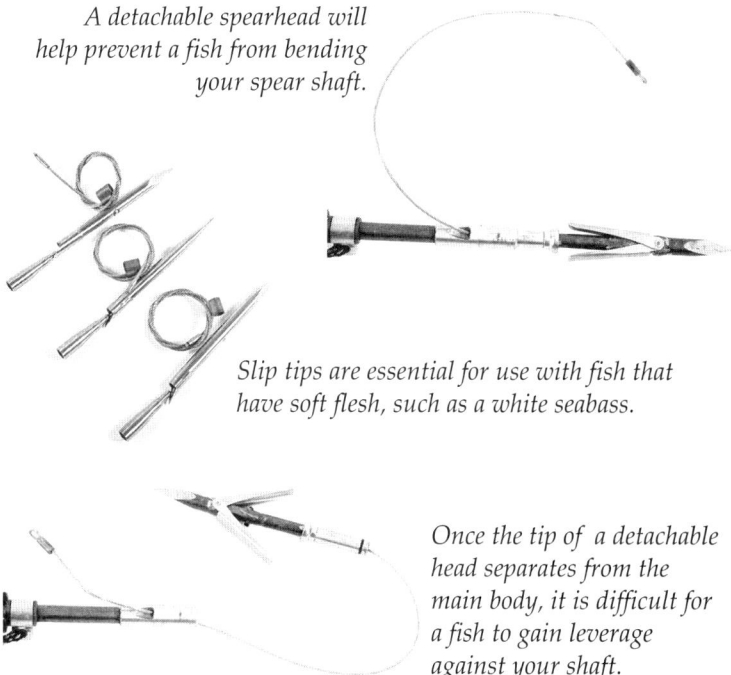

A detachable spearhead will help prevent a fish from bending your spear shaft.

Slip tips are essential for use with fish that have soft flesh, such as a white seabass.

Once the tip of a detachable head separates from the main body, it is difficult for a fish to gain leverage against your shaft.

Spearfishing Accessories

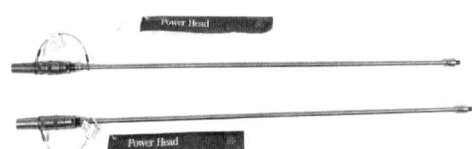

Powerheads are firearms and are not considered acceptable spearfishing equipment. They must be used as defensive weapons only.

your equipment if handled improperly, even when they have not been fired from a gun. You must use caution to avoid personal injury and to avoid injuring other divers around you.

POWERHEADS

Powerheads are <u>not</u> considered gear for recreational spearfishing. The powerhead is primarily used as a defensive weapon when working in the water with aggressive sharks.

Powerheads use conventional topside ammunition in a special underwater mechanism attached to a polespear. The ammunition will normally be treated with a waterproof coating. The head may be spring loaded and there is a firing pin to detonate the ammunition.

Powerheads are extremely dangerous in the hands of the inexperienced user. They must be treated as lethal weapons.

SPEAR SHAFTS

Spear shafts are primarily selected according to the length of gun that you use, although the diameter of the shaft may be varied according to your hunting activity. As explained previously, if you are going after big fish you will want a heavier shaft. However, smaller shafts can move through the water faster and you must balance your need for penetration against speed and your personal accuracy. A perfectly placed shot that gets the penetration you need is the ideal.

All spearshafts are made from high quality stainless steel. They must be notched at the trigger end for the particular mechanism used in your gun and threaded to accept your spear tip. They also must be notched to provide the connection between the shaft and the bands. Riffe's spear shafts have a series of raised projections welded to them, rather than notches, to provide a place to connect the bands for cocking the gun.

Popular shaft diameters include 5/16 inch, 3/8 inch, and 9/32 inch. If you select a heavier shaft for your existing gun, you must be sure that the gun is designed to handle it. For the gun to perform well with a larger shaft you will probably need to replace your bands with heavier bands.

BANDS

The bands used on all band powered guns are actually made from surgical tubing. Tubing is measured by its outer diameter and comes in a variety of thicknesses as well as materials. The heavier and thicker the tubing, the more power it will have to propel the spear, but this will also make the bands more difficult to pull.

Black surgical tubing is primarily made from synthetic rubber. Amber surgical tubing is made from a natural rubber and is generally considered to have more "snap".

Some bands use stainless steel "wishbones" to engage the notches in the spear shaft. The wishbones must be bent at precisely the right angle to engage the shaft and provide the proper propulsion. Other bands, such as those provided by Riffe, use nylon line to provide the connecting point between the bands and shaft. Some divers prefer nylon "wishbones" to stainless wishbones because they feel they make less noise when the gun is fired and are less likely to scare fish. Wishbones may be attached to the tubing by using either a ring or by tying them tightly with heavy duty nylon thread.

Speargun bands are made from surgical tubing.

If you want to get more power from your existing gun you can usually switch to a heavier set of bands. However, you must check with the manufacturer of your gun to verify its maximum capacity.

LINES AND SHOCK CORDS

Since most speared fish don't die immediately, even when you get a good shot, a line connected between the spear and your gun is essential to prevent the loss of the fish. The line must be rugged enough to withstand repeated chafing from rocks, barnacles, and other abrasive elements found underwater.

The most common type of line used is white nylon, usually 1/8 inch or 3/16 inch. Riffe offers a Kevlar® line that provides an excellent strength to weight ratio. Divers also use monofilament and "tuna line", a braided nylon with a special chemical coating that makes it more durable.

The line is normally strung from the front of the gun or muzzle, to the line release mechanism that is actuated by the trigger. The line is commonly tied to the front tip of the gun using a bowline. The other end of the line is attached to a stainless steel "slider", or the fin on the shaft if your gun uses this design. If you are using a reel, the line will normally be attached from the slider (or the fin) directly to the reel.

Most spearguns are provided with a length of shock cord integrated with the line. The purpose of the shock cord is primarily to

Your gun should be strung with a line appropriate to the fish you plan to hunt. For most ordinary applications, braided nylon provides the best compromise between durability and economy.

Some free divers use a torpedo buoy attached to their line to prevent a fish from running away with their gun. This is one alternative to using a reel.

make it easy to fasten the line to the gun by giving it stretch. It only minimally helps to take out the jolt of the initial run of the fish.

Some spearfishermen who primarily free dive often use extended lines attached to a torpedo buoy or other surface float, rather than a reel. The line floats on the surface and trails behind the diver as he swims along. The buoy prevents a fish from diving and running away with your gun.

Instead of using an ordinary nylon line with a torpedo buoy a more popular method of fastening the buoy to a speargun is to use a nylon line that is installed in flexible plastic tubing. These lines are called "float lines". The advantage to this arrangement is that the line is far less likely to tangle than nylon line spooling off a reel. The disadvantage to this method of rigging your gun is that the line floats and in areas of heavy boat traffic you run the risk of a boat running over your line. If this happens you could lose your gun, cause damage to the boat, or be personally injured if you become tangled in the line.

In the Gulf of Mexico, it is not uncommon for divers who do their spearfishing on offshore oil platforms to use stainless steel wire in place of nylon line on their spearguns. The vertical relief of these platforms combined with the razor sharp marine growth that is found on them can quickly cut any ordinary line.

REELS

When a large and powerful fish runs, it can easily jerk your gun out of your hands in its initial charge if your spear is connected to the gun only by a short length of line. By attaching a reel, you have a place to spool enough line for the fish to make a fairly long run without giving you a strong jolt. Even if the fish still has power after its long initial run, the line creates drag that will help tire the fish out. In addition, the fish must take the slack out of the line and stretch it before it makes a direct pull on you.

Reels have the added benefit of allowing you to give a fish enough line to help avoid having it tear the tip out of its body, if your shaft did not get complete penetration. By allowing the fish to wear itself out against the drag of the line this makes it easier and safer to string your fish.

In ordinary fishing, the reel is used to fight the fish and reel it back to the boat. There is no leverage to fight the fish the way speargun reels are rigged. Once the fish has stopped swimming, you use the reel line to follow and find the fish.

Some scuba divers will use line from the reel to tow a speared and subdued fish a distance of up to 30 feet behind them underwater. They prefer this technique over having a speared fish on a stringer right next to their body. There are problems with this method, too, especially entanglement of your line as well as exposing the fish to predators.

If you plan to spear large fish and freedive, a reel or some other arrangement for extended line is essential if you make a poor shot on a large fish. Without some additional line, there would be no way for you to surface and keep track of the fish.

Most speargun reels are made from a combination of plastic, and/or aluminum and stainless steel. The reel should be equipped with a drag, to help prevent the line from unwinding accidentally, not necessarily to slow down the fish. Most reels are equipped with their own release mechanism to also help prevent the reel from paying out line unintentionally.

If you spear a large fish and your shot is not good, you must be immediately prepared to release the line on your reel. However, sometimes a fish will bolt so quickly that it is impossible to operate the release. For this reason, many blue water spearfishermen who go after large fish remove the release from their reels. They depend solely on the drag to keep the line on the reel.

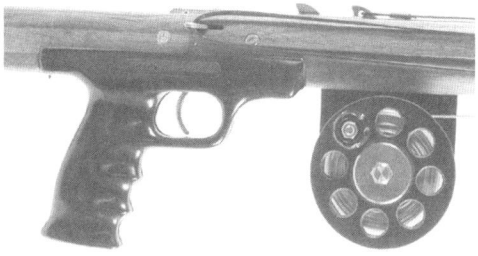

If you plan to hunt large fish, a reel is another way to rig your gun. This reel is manufactured by Riffe.

Keep in mind that any accessories that you add to the gun, such as a reel, will change its buoyancy and will affect the flotation of the gun. While most spearguns are designed to float when the shaft is out of the gun, it may not behave this way if you have added the weight of a reel.

BREAKAWAY GEAR

Another method that free divers sometimes use to ensure that they don't lose a large, powerful fish is to use a system known as "breakaway gear". This is a system that usually includes a long length of line as well as an inflatable buoy. The entire system mounts in a plastic tube that is fastened underneath the barrel of the speargun.

Breakaway gear used to be very popular back in the late sixties and early seventies, but it is less commonly seen today. Breakaway gear is somewhat bulky.

GUN BAGS

If you have a wooden speargun, particularly if it is a custom gun, you'll want to protect it to keep it in good condition. A padded gun bag is a good investment to extend the life of your gun, especially if you do much travel.

Gun bags are available in a variety of materials, but the two most popular are nylon and neoprene. Better gun bags have pockets to hold spare tips and compartments to hold additional shafts, separate from the gun compartment.

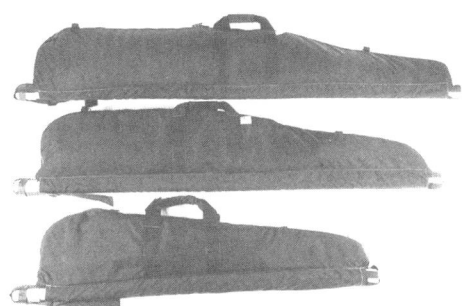

To protect your speargun during travel, a gun bag is essential. These bags were made by the Blue Water Hunter dive shop in Goleta, California.

You can use a flashlight to locate fish hiding in holes.

FLASHLIGHTS

Although most novice spearfishermen wouldn't think of a flashlight as a tool for locating fish, a flashlight can be indispensable. Flashlights are especially valuable if you dive around wrecks, rock or coral reefs. Many species of fish will hide in holes in these structures and without a flashlight you won't be able to see them.

Most spearfishermen prefer the smallest flashlight possible that will still provide a decent amount of light. Larger flashlights, such as those used for lobster diving, are too big and bulky to be handled easily when you are also carrying a speargun.

Flashlights are not considered an acceptable light source for spearfishing at night. In most locations, spearfishing at night is illegal, since some fish will sleep at night. Spearfishing at night is not considered a sportsmanlike activity and can be extremely dangerous for other divers in the area. Never spear fish at night.

STRINGERS

There are many different types of stringers available to carry your fish with you underwater. The first big issue you must

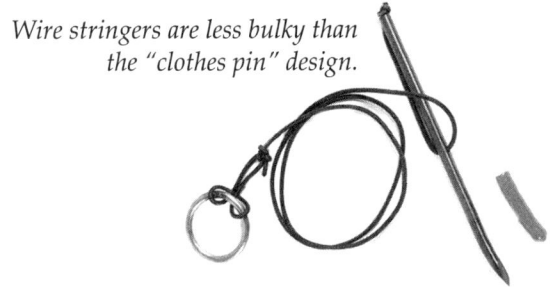

Wire stringers are less bulky than the "clothes pin" design.

Some divers feel that this "clothes pin" stringer design is more secure than the wire stringer.

decide is whether you want to string fish or not. The obvious danger in carrying bleeding, struggling fish is that you may attract sharks or other predators.

Many spearfishermen in certain parts of the world have used stringers underwater successfully for years without a problem. Yet there are certain areas where stringing fish is definitely a poor idea, such as the Farallon Islands off California, where there is a large population of white sharks.

Stringing fish always presents a certain element of risk, any time you dive in ocean waters. To increase your safety, get your catch out of the water as quickly as possible.

The two main types of stringers are those that work like a giant safety pin and those that are made from stainless wire (or

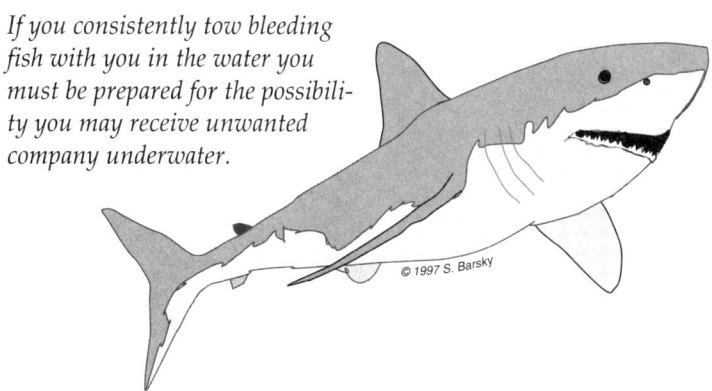

If you consistently tow bleeding fish with you in the water you must be prepared for the possibility you may receive unwanted company underwater.

Spearfishing Accessories

monofilament) with a large stainless pin on the end. Both types are designed to feed through the fish's eyes or through the gills and out the mouth.

Divers who prefer the clothes pin design generally feel that they are more positive and secure, and that you are less likely to lose a fish when using them. Those that prefer the stainless wire and pin design generally feel that they are less cumbersome, quieter, and it is somewhat easier to string a fish using this design.

There are numerous variations on both designs and you may need to try more than one stringer to find the one that works best for you. You may also find that you prefer different stringers under different situations. Some divers modify their stringers to use a soft line such as braided nylon rather than stainless steel wire to avoid cutting through the flesh of a soft fish and losing it.

Whichever stringer you choose, it must be attached to your belt in such a way that you can release it instantly if you need to do so. Most divers use a brass snap hook for this purpose.

KNIVES

While every diver should carry a knife for safety underwater, the spearfisherman may want several different types of knives. The general purpose diver's knife is normally used for cutting line or kelp, prying scallops off rocks, and other similar chores. However, most spearfishermen will want to carry a sharp, narrow blade knife that is used primarily to kill wounded fish and

A short, sharp knife is useful to help stop a fish from struggling after it has been speared.

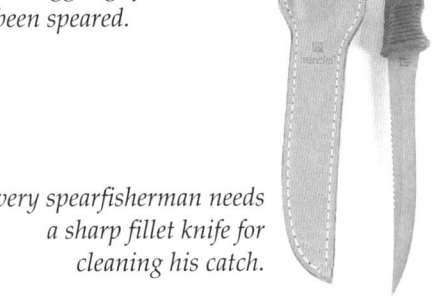

Every spearfisherman needs a sharp fillet knife for cleaning his catch.

stop their struggling. Many underwater hunters choose a stiletto or small dagger for this purpose. The knife must also be able to cut the spearfishing line in the event that it becomes hopelessly entangled in a wreck or reef and the diver is unable to free it.

The spearfisherman's knife must have a narrow enough blade to easily penetrate flesh and cut through a fish's spine or skull. However, the blade must also be sturdy enough to bend a bit without snapping off.

The Dive-Alert™ should be part of your dive gear if you scuba dive in remote locations.

Spearfishing knives are generally worn on the leg or the weight belt, attached to the buoyancy compensator harness, or may even be worn on the arm. It depends on your personal preference.

In addition to your spearfishing knife, every spearfisherman will need a good quality fillet knife for cleaning his catch. Without a razor sharp knife you will waste a good deal of the meat on your catch. Most good fillet knives have thin blades that are at least ten inches long.

FLARES AND OTHER SIGNALLING DEVICES

Anytime that you dive at a remote location, particularly where there are strong currents, it is essential that you carry some type of signaling device that you can use to attract attention. It is extremely difficult for a diver to be seen in the water at the surface, particularly when the conditions are rough. No matter how loud you shout, it is hard to get someone's attention when you are even a short distance away, and almost impossible to be heard above the sound of the wind or a boat's motor.

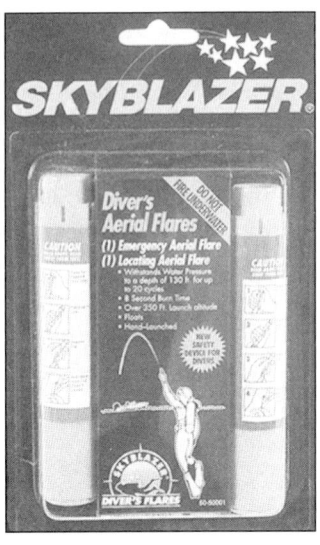

Flares are useful for signaling to vessels that are far away, beyond the reach of sound.

Ideally, you should carry both sound signaling devices as well as visual devices for attracting attention if you need help in the water. Sound signaling devices include air powered horns and whistles, while visual devices include flares, stainless steel mirrors, and inflatable tubes such as Scuba Tuba™.

Probably the most effective air powered horn for divers is the Dive-Alert™ manufactured by Ideations. This device plugs into the hose that supplies your power inflator and provides an extremely loud signal that can be heard at long distances. If you regularly dive at offshore locations this item is essential.

Whistles can also be effective signaling devices, although they don't have nearly the range that the Dive-Alert™ horn offers. If you carry a whistle, you must be sure that it is rustproof and designed to withstand the marine environment.

The most effective visual signals include flares and inflatable devices like Scuba-Tuba™. The Skyblazer® flares are designed to go underwater, but are strictly for signaling topside. Like all flares these devices can cause severe burns and start fires if used improperly. Flares generally can be seen from a greater distance than any other type of visual device.

All flares have a "shelf-life", a date beyond which they lose their reliability and ultimately, their ability to properly ignite. For this reason, flares must be replaced whenever they reach the date that is stamped on them.

Inflatable signaling devices, such as Scuba Tuba™ or some of the inflatable nylon buoys that are available are another method of attracting attention if you are in the water, far from shore. Some of the better devices on the market are completely sealed and have a stem type oral inflator tube.

Stainless steel mirrors are probably the least effective visual signaling devices, since the sun must be shining and the sea must be relatively calm for them to work well. It is difficult to carry a large enough mirror to be effective at a distance. The advantage to using a mirror is that there are no moving parts and nothing to corrode.

Sharpening Stone and File

To keep your spearheads and knives in top condition you will want to carry a file for the heads and a stone or sharpening steel for your knives. These items can be carried in a small tackle box along with your other accessories and spares.

A file is essential to keeping your spear tips sharp. Even if you don't ever shoot rocks, if you are a good shot, the bones you hit inside the fish you spear will eventually dull your tip. A file will help restore the point and you may want to use the stone itself for final sharpening.

Spare Parts

Always carry enough spare parts and tools with you on the boat or to the beach to keep your gear functional so you don't ruin a dive trip. A partial list of spare parts and tools that you should carry would include the following:

- Selection of spearheads
- Loctite® 222 Small Screw Threadlocker
- Caps or sheaths for spearheads
- 25 feet of 1/8 inch or 3/16 inch white nylon
- Matches
- 3 feet of stainless steel wire for your detachable spearhead
- Wire rope swage fittings
- Swaging tool
- Spare bands for your gun

Spearfishing Accessories

- WD-40®
- Spare snap hooks
- Swivels (if your gun is rigged with them)
- Pliers
- Side cutters
- Phillips head screwdriver
- Flat blade screwdriver
- 6 inch adjustable wrench

The accessories listed in this chapter are some of the more important and useful ones that will make your spearfishing more productive and safer. There are many others. Check with your dive store to see what items are most useful in your area.

CHAPTER 4

FREEDIVING GEAR

For the purists who spear fish by freediving, specialized equipment has evolved, primarily in Italy, France, and Portugal, that makes underwater hunting easier and more enjoyable. This gear includes low volume masks, long blade fins, "dry" snorkels, and freediving wetsuits. Taken together, these items can make you a more efficient underwater predator.

LOW VOLUME MASKS

Low volume masks have always been popular with freedivers because they require very little air from your lungs to equalize the pressure inside the mask as you dive. They also require very little air to clear them should any water get inside.

The masks that have the lowest volume are almost like goggles in appearance, with two separate lenses held in one plane by a hard plastic frame. They achieve their low volume by placing the frame for the lens directly against your forehead while providing a rubber pocket for your nose that sticks out beyond the lenses.

There are several side benefits that are achieved by using a low volume mask. First, these masks tend to be lighter weight than other masks, and secondly, because they have a lower profile they have less drag, which allows you to move through the water more efficiently.

Select a mask for freediving just as you would for scuba diving. Test the fit by placing the mask against your face, inhale, and hold your breath. The mask must stick in place due to the suction alone. If the mask leaks, the fit is unsatisfactory. However, even if the mask fits, you must also be sure that the mask will be comfortable to wear for extended periods of time while you are in the water. Any mask that you select for freediving will usually be suitable for scuba diving as well.

Some freedivers prefer a medium volume mask rather than a low volume mask. Their rationale is that they can inhale the air from the mask to give themselves perhaps another twenty seconds while ascending. This is considered an advanced technique and **not** something that should be attempted by the novice diver.

Low volume masks for spearfishing are available from companies such as Beuchat, Cressi, Sporasub, and Mares. These companies all specialize in gear for freediving.

Low volume masks are preferred by most serious freedivers.

Dry Snorkels

When I was a boy, my first snorkel had a "J" shape at both the top and the bottom, with a ping pong ball in a cage on the top. The ping pong ball was supposed to keep the water out of the snorkel when you submerged, so you could start breathing right away when you surfaced. As anyone who has ever tried one of these snorkels knows, they didn't work at all, and serious divers were warned against snorkels with any extra devices attached to them.

Several years ago U.S. Divers Co., Inc. introduced the Impulse® snorkel, a revolutionary design with an upper annular valve that automatically vents any water that enters the snorkel while the diver swims on the surface. Like most experienced divers, when I first saw the Impulse® I was dubious, but I quickly found it to be one of the best snorkels I had ever used. Other companies that have produced popular "dry" snorkels include TUSA, Dacor, Ocean Master, Oceanic, and others.

The Impulse® remains one of the most successful dry snorkels on the market because it combines ease of use without creating significant additional breathing resistance. It makes surface swimming in choppy water easy, because you don't need to clear your snorkel every

A good snorkel makes freediving and surface swimming much easier. This Impulse® snorkel from U.S. Divers is extremely popular.

time a wave splashes water into it. For freediving, it helps to vent most of the water when you surface from a breath-hold dive. Before you purchase any dry snorkel, be sure to test how it breathes and see if it is satisfactory for you.

Ideally, the breathing section of a good snorkel should not be longer than eighteen inches in length and should have no sharp bends. If the snorkel has a corrugated hose the inside of the tube must be smooth or the breathing resistance of the snorkel will be unacceptably high.

Although the dry snorkels are all somewhat bulkier than ordinary snorkels, they more than make up for their drag underwater with their superior performance on the surface. For extended surface swimming, a dry snorkel is definitely a preferred piece of equipment.

LONG BLADE FINS

Long blade fins have been popular in Europe for many years, but have only become popular in the U.S. in the past five years. Most of the long blade fins are more than ten inches longer than the standard fins used for scuba diving. Among the more popular designs are those from Beuchat, Cressi Sub, Esclapez, and Picasso. Bob Evans Design/Force Fins in the U.S. also markets a long blade fin that is excellent for freediving.

Unlike the open heel adjustable fins used for scuba diving, the majority of long blade fins are sold as full foot fins. The divers who use these fins in colder waters normally wear them with wetsuit socks or "shooter booties", with a soft sole.

Stiff long blade fins require substantially more effort to kick than do conventional fins. If you aren't in great shape, it takes time to build up to using stiff fins for a full day of diving.

Be sure to try several different sets of long blade fins before you settle on a final purchase. There is no one best pair of fins, because every diver has a different anatomy and the performance of a pair of fins is directly influenced by the length of your thigh, calf, and overall leg length. The characteristics of each brand of fins are quite different, and you need to see which pair works best for you. What works for your buddy may not work well for you.

ANKLE WEIGHTS AND FIN WEIGHTS

One of the goals of the serious freediver is to try to be as silent as possible while moving through the water to avoid scaring any potential prey away from your area. In order to achieve

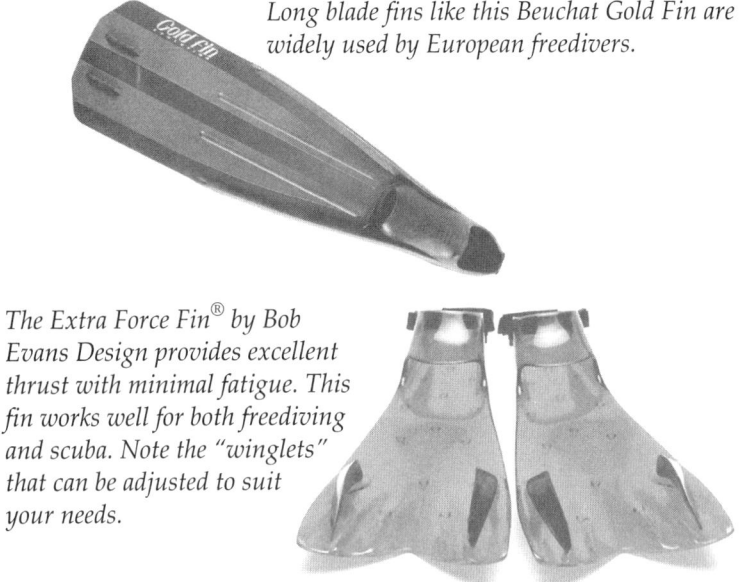

Long blade fins like this Beuchat Gold Fin are widely used by European freedivers.

The Extra Force Fin® by Bob Evans Design provides excellent thrust with minimal fatigue. This fin works well for both freediving and scuba. Note the "winglets" that can be adjusted to suit your needs.

this goal, it's essential not to splash any water when you are kicking on the surface.

Some freedivers wear ankle weights or use fin weights to help make their fin movements more quiet. The weights help to keep their fins below the surface. Any time your fins break the surface, the noise of your fins slapping against the water may be enough to frighten any game fish that are nearby. The ankle weights have an added benefit of helping you to swim more efficiently on the surface, since any time your fins break the surface they are not helping to propel you through the water.

Ankle weights come in a wide variety of configurations and weights. However, the most common ankle weight designs employ plastic Fastex® buckles and the weights do not exceed more than a pound and a half.

Ankle weights can be used to help keep your legs "down" and your fins from breaking the surface and splashing.

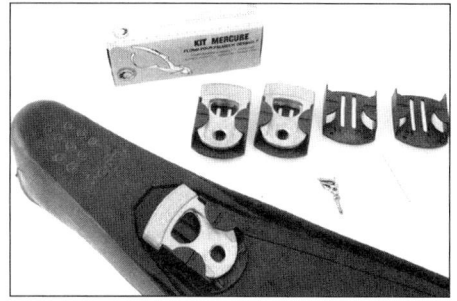

Some divers prefer fin weights to ankle weights.

One of the problems with ankle weights is that by placing a weight out at the end of your leg you are increasing the stress on your lower back. Some divers find that they cannot use ankle weights without experiencing lower back pain. If this is a problem for you, discontinue any use of ankle weights.

If you do decide to use ankle weights, be sure to remove a corresponding amount of weight from your weight belt. For freediving it is better for your buoyancy to be slightly positive rather than slightly negative.

Another way to add weight to help keep your fins from breaking the surface is to use fin weights. Fin weights generally attach to the bottom of the fins and work in a manner similar to ankle weights.

Freediving Wetsuits

To freedive and hunt effectively in cold water you will probably want a wetsuit that is designed a bit differently than those used for scuba diving. You will find that you can usually use a suit that is a bit thinner than what you would use for scuba diving.

The advantage to a thinner suit is that it will be less restrictive and will give you more freedom of movement and flexibility. Since almost half your time in the water is spent on the surface rather than at depth, you can get away with a thinner suit than you would need for scuba diving. However, if you spend long periods of time in the water, you will need a suit that is thick enough to keep you warm after you have been in the water for a few hours.

Most freedivers order their suits with single sided nylon on the exterior of the suit, and a smooth rubber "skin" on

A waist seal will help to cut down on water circulation inside your suit.

the inside. Another type of "skin in" suit material utilizes a honeycomb cell surface on the inside of the suit. These materials offer better warmth and flexibility than nylon two-sided material. No matter which of these two materials you select, you must use either talcum powder, corn starch, or a dilute solution of hair conditioner to don suits made from these materials.

If you dive in cold water be sure that your suit includes an attached hood, and wear gloves and boots. These are all high heat

Wear a hood if you dive in cold water to help prevent heat loss from your head.

loss areas that must be kept warm. You can lose up to 50% of your body heat from your head if it is unprotected, so be sure to get a hood that fits properly.

Unless you have a perfect physique (which is rare), you will probably want a custom made wetsuit. Most people cannot get an adequate fit from an off-the-rack suit. If at all possible, make the effort to travel to the suit maker's facility so that the person who cuts the suit has the opportunity to measure you. This will help ensure the best possible fit.

A proper fitting wetsuit should be snug, but not excessively tight. There should be no loose bulges anywhere in the suit. Check with other divers in your area to see who is the most popular custom suit maker with local hunters.

Some of the options that you may want on your suit include a cocking pad for loading your gun, a knife pocket, and seals on the wrist, ankles, face, and waist. These options will help to make your hunting more comfortable and enjoyable.

Suits for freediving are normally as thin as possible, consistent with the water temperature and your individual thermal needs.

Freediving Gear

Not everyone can use a cocking pad comfortably, so try this option out before ordering one for your suit. Many divers still find that placing a band gun against their weight belt buckle is the most comfortable position for cocking it. For a pneumatic gun, the only possible cocking positions are to support the gun on the top of your thigh or foot.

For the freediver, a knife pocket is an excellent suit option, since it will help streamline your suit. The knife is still stored in its sheath, but the entire sheath is slipped into the pocket, minus the straps. You are also less likely to lose your knife when it is held in place in a pocket rather than a sheath on your leg.

In cold water, your suit should be equipped with either a pair of farmer john style pants or with a waist seal. The advantage to the farmer john is that you have a double layer of insulation on your torso. Yet, some divers find the farmer john to be a bit restrictive and prefer the waist seal.

The waist seal is an extra flap of rubber that is located on the inside of the jacket. To use the waist seal, once you have donned your pants and jacket, you fold up the bottom of your jacket and fold down the top of your pants. Folding up the jacket exposes the waist seal whose end is normally flush with the bottom end of your jacket. The top of the high waisted pants is then pulled up so that it covers the waist seal. The jacket is then rolled down. This triple layer of rubber then helps to prevent water movement through the suit. However, the waist seal does not provide as much insulation for your chest and vital organs.

Additional seals on the wrists, ankles, and hood all help to reduce water movement through your suit. These seals are normally just a strip of "skin in" rubber (no nylon) located at the end of the arms and ankles of the suit, as well as around the opening for the face.

Rubber Weight Belts

Serious freedivers prefer rubber weight belts or other depth compensated belts that don't move to help reduce the amount of noise a sliding weight belt and weights create underwater.

Without a depth compensated belt, as your suit compresses, your belt will shift around on your body. A weight belt that moves creates noise as the belt slips, whether you are freediving or scuba diving. On a scuba diver, a sliding belt can be especially noisy if the weights or buckle bang against your tank.

The other major advantage to a depth compensated belt is that the buckle normally remains in the exact position where you fastened it. This is an important safety factor, especially if you ever need to ditch your belt in a hurry. Searching for a belt buckle in order to release it is not acceptable in an emergency situation.

To use a depth compensated belt, you tighten the belt before you dive and as your suit compresses the belt adjusts for that compression.

Rubber weight belts stretch and are less likely to create noise underwater since they tend to stay in position.

Notes

CHAPTER 5

WHERE TO FIND FISH

Most fish, with the exception of open ocean (i.e., pelagic) species are normally found around underwater structures, including wrecks, coral reefs, rock reefs, and kelp forests. These habitats provide fish with a place to hide and, as other animals are attracted to the same structures, a place to feed. In many cases, underwater structures also act as a haven for fish that are breeding and a hiding place for eggs or larvae. The more you know about different types of habitat and fish species, the more successful you will be as an underwater hunter.

Before you start spearfishing in a new area, be sure to check local regulations to ensure that you are within the law. For example, along the west coast of the U.S. there are different regulations that apply to the different islands, as well as laws that vary in different parts of the state. In California in particular, there are prohibitions regarding how close you can hunt near the opening of a creek, stream, or river.

It is your responsibility to investigate what laws pertain in each area. As far as game wardens are concerned, ignorance of the law is no excuse. In some places your dive gear and even your boat may be seized. In addition, there are frequently stiff fines for these violations. You must know the law that applies to the species you wish to hunt.

FRESH WATER LAKES AND RIVERS

There are few states where you can spear fish in fresh water, and even in those places where you can, the number of species is normally severely restricted. For example, no state will allow you

Most fresh water lakes have muddy bottoms that are easily stirred up, dramatically reducing visibility.

to hunt anadromous fishes (those that can live in both fresh and salt water) such as salmon or steelhead trout. In fact, various populations of steelhead trout were listed as endangered species in 1996 in Oregon, Washington, and California.

States that will allow you to spear fish in fresh water will generally only allow you to hunt for "rough" fish, such as catfish or pike. Be sure to check on the restrictions in the area where you intend to hunt.

Many of the lakes and rivers where you can spear fish have muddy bottoms that can be easily stirred up. Extra care must be taken in these environments to avoid reducing your visibility.

Submerged trees are another hazard that you must be alert for in any lake or river. Many lakes that are man-made have numerous submerged trees that were on the site before the lake was flooded. These trees can snag your equipment, but they also may provide habitat for fish.

Trees that have fallen into rivers can move along with great speed. They can definitely be hazardous to your health if you get in the way of one.

Salt Water Habitats

There are numerous types of salt water habitats, including sandy bottoms, rocky reefs, kelp forests, coral reefs, and man-made structures. Each different type of habitat is home to particular species of fishes that require their own hunting techniques.

Sandy Bottoms

Most of the hunting that takes place along sandy bottoms involves scouting for flatfish, such as the peacock flounder found off Florida. Probably the biggest danger of hunting along a sandy bottom is that you may die of terminal boredom. If you hunt for the California halibut you may spend many hours swimming over a featureless bottom without seeing a fish.

Most sandy bottoms are boring places, with few features of interest. The exception to this is when the squid come into shallow water off California to spawn during the spring months. Many types of marine life, including halibut, come into sandy coves to feed on the squid and the resulting swarm of marine life is impressive.

Hunting on sandy bottoms usually poses few problems for the diver, other than the possibility of failing to check your depth as the bottom slopes away. Currents can also be a problem when you hunt on an exposed stretch of sand, since there are no obstructions to block their flow. Don't let the distractions of hunting keep you from closely monitoring your bottom time, depth, and location relative to the boat or shore.

Rocky Bottom

Rocky bottoms are one of the most common habitats where you will find fish in colder waters. Like all good fish habitats it provides shelter for both juvenile and adult fish as well as many other creatures.

Look for fish in rocky habitats near the bottom, but also in holes, crevices, and caverns. If you regularly hunt in this type of terrain you will find a small flashlight is useful to help you look back into holes. However, you must avoid penetrating caverns or caves that are not open to direct sunlight.

The temptation to go into a cave or cavern entrance can be great, especially if you are "fired up" for the hunt. Keep in mind that while fish will frequently enter a cavern where they can see light, it is unusual to find large fish back inside a marine underwater cave. Never enter a cave or cavern unless you have trained for this type of diving. Besides the direct hazards of getting lost inside a cavern or cave, it would be extremely difficult to practice proper cave diving techniques and subdue a struggling fish at the same time.

Just because you have been trained in cave or cavern diving doesn't mean the fish that you spear inside a cave will observe the same rules of cave diving etiquette. Most fish have never even heard of cave diver training or any of the cave diving organizations. You can count on a speared fish doing everything it can to get away, including stirring up the bottom inside a cave or cavern.

Low lying rocks are usually not nearly as good a habitat as bottom where you have dramatic relief, where there are rocks that rise many feet up off the bottom. The more holes and spaces between the rocks, the better the habitat is for fish. You will need a flashlight for looking into holes and caverns to locate fish in these structures.

There are few natural hazards on rocky bottoms that you need be concerned about. Probably the biggest danger to enthusiastic spearfisherman is the sea urchin, which can puncture both wetsuits and dry suits.

If you do shoot a fish in a hole be sure you have a good, clean shot. Many divers have lost spear shafts due to fish wedging themselves in holes where the diver cannot reach the shaft. In these situations, your only alternative may be to cut the line connecting the shaft to the gun.

It is also possible for a large fish to bend your shaft by wedging itself into a hole. Although you may be

Rock reefs are normally productive hunting grounds.

able to free the fish, retrieving it and the shaft, bent shafts can't always be straightened enough to be used again.

Rocky reefs are normally found in cold or temperate water diving areas. In colder waters in particular, you will not find the diversity of species that is found in warmer waters, but you will find greater numbers of individuals of the same species.

The interface between a rock reef and a sand bottom can also be a productive area to hunt. On the west coast of the U.S., for example, it is not uncommon to find halibut lying in the sand on the fringe of a rocky reef.

Man-made artificial rock reefs are frequently made from demolished bridges or rubble from other concrete structures. There have also been reefs made from pre-fabricated cast concrete structures. These sites quickly take on the characteristics of a natural rock reef and make good hunting grounds.

KELP FORESTS

On the west coast of the U.S. the kelp forests are among the most beautiful and productive habitats in which to hunt. Many different species of fish can be found in the kelp forests, including calico bass, white seabass, rockfish, and other species.

The canopy of a kelp forest is a beautiful place to hunt for fish.

Unlike hunting in a forest on land, kelp forests undergo rapid, dynamic changes from week to week. A site that has a thick, lush kelp forest one month may be almost devoid of kelp when the water warms up or following a strong Pacific storm.

Kelp forests can be difficult places to hunt, especially when the kelp is thick. When the kelp is thickly matted on the surface, your movement through the canopy can be quite restricted.

Whenever you hunt in kelp you must be sure to leave yourself enough air to return to the boat or beach by swimming underneath the kelp. Swimming on the surface through kelp is especially difficult if you are carrying a speargun and trailing a stringer of speared fish.

CORAL REEFS

Coral reefs are another type of structure where you will find many different species of fish. Like rock reefs, fish are attracted by both the shelter and food that they can find on a coral reef.

While large fish may be found almost anywhere on a coral reef, deep drop-off areas tend to be a good place to find larger

Coral reefs provide shelter to a wide variety of fish and animals.

fish, particularly pelagics such as amberjacks. These fish will often come in from deep water to the edge of the reef to feed.

On coral reefs that have holes, tunnels, and crevices, look for fish that may be hiding in these areas. Warm water species are just as likely to hide as cold water fish.

It is especially important when you hunt on coral reefs that you take extra care not to damage the coral or other marine creatures. Coral is extremely slow growing and easily broken.

If you dive in a warm water area that is known to have many species of sharks present, it is wise to get your catch out of the water as soon as possible. There is no sense in waving dinner in front of a potentially dangerous animal if you can avoid it.

Before planning any tropical dive trip or spearfishing in any tropical area, be sure to thoroughly investigate the local laws that apply. Most resort destinations will not permit you to hunt at popular dive sites.

BlueWater Hunting

Bluewater hunting is among the most challenging spearfishing practiced today. It is usually performed only by serious freedivers working out in deep water. Most bluewater hunting is done along the edges of deep reefs or drop-offs, in warm and temperate waters.

The usual targets sought by bluewater hunters are fish like wahoo, tuna, yellowtail, and dolphin (dorado). Hunting these fish normally requires large powerful spearguns.

Shipwrecks

Like rocky bottoms and coral reefs, shipwrecks provide good habitat for many different species of fish, no matter where the wreck is located. The more intact the wreck, the more places there are for fish to hide.

The main hazards on shipwrecks are the sharp metal found on decaying steel hulls and the possibility of entrapment. As shipwrecks fall apart, the metal tears and twists, leaving razor sharp edges that can cut through your suit, your skin, and your speargun line.

It would be highly unlikely to find any fish worth spearing deep inside a wreck. Most of the fish you will find on a wreck

Shipwrecks attract fish and provide a good place to hunt.

will be in open passages or compartments, or swimming around the perimeter of the wreck, so avoid entering a wreck to look for fish. Like the hazards associated with cave diving, becoming lost or disoriented inside a wreck can be a fatal experience. Never penetrate a wreck unless you have been specifically trained for this type of diving and have all the proper equipment. Just as it would be nearly impossible to subdue a struggling fish inside a cave while still following proper cave diving procedures, the same holds true for wreck diving.

Besides the possibility of getting lost inside a wreck, another danger is that older wrecks can collapse due to the stress created by trapped scuba air pushing upwards inside a compartment. Ships are not built to take internal pressure and as a diver's exhaled air accumulates inside a cabin or passageway it can create lift and a strain on the structural integrity of the ship. There has been more than one accident where a wreck has caved in on itself due to the upward lift created by a diver's bubbles. This type of incident has resulted in diving fatalities.

OFFSHORE OIL PLATFORMS

Offshore oil platforms provide good habitat for fish and other marine creatures. Most platforms are covered with mussels, starfish, barnacles, and other invertebrates. These animals provide food for some species of fish, and the structures themselves provide hiding places for fish.

Common offshore platforms are normally square or rectangular in shape, with large vertical "legs" at each of their four corners. Numerous structural cross members are strung between each of these legs at regular depth intervals from above the surface down to the bottom.

Many offshore platforms sit in deep water, miles from shore. When you dive these structures, you will frequently only be diving the top levels of the structure. This is where the water will be the clearest and the most life will be seen. Rarely will you ever dive the bottom of an offshore oil platform. If you drop something at a shallower depth, unless you swim fast or are lucky and it lands on a shallow cross member, you will probably never see it again if it falls away into deep water.

Offshore oil platforms are often located far offshore and frequently attract pelagic species.

There are numerous hazards to diving offshore oil platforms and you should not dive these structures until you have been provided an orientation to them by a knowledgeable local instructor. Some of the hazards you can expect to encounter include heavy boat traffic, electric shock, suction pipes, entanglement, and falling objects.

Most oil companies now require that you get permission prior to diving on any offshore oil structure. These companies are extremely wary of the liability problems that may arise if someone is killed or injured diving on one of their structures. This is a reasonable concern on their part.

In most cases, you will not be permitted to tie up to an oil platform. These platforms are working facilities that receive a constant stream of boat traffic for incoming and outbound personnel, as well as supplies. Equipment and personnel may be loaded onto the platform from all sides, and a small boat that's in the way may mean costly delays as well as the potential for an accident. Never tie up to an offshore platform unless you have permission to do so.

Anchoring near offshore oil platforms may also pose a problem as there are frequently numerous submerged oil and natural gas pipelines. If you damage a pipeline with your anchor you could be liable for hundreds of thousands of dollars in lost revenues for the oil company, as well as environmental fines from the Coast Guard and other government agencies if there is an oil spill.

In many cases, divers who have permission to dive an offshore oil structure will "live boat" where one team of divers stays aboard the boat while a second team enters the water. The boat is never anchored, but is positioned down current from the structure to keep an eye out for the divers. When the first team completes their dive, the boat is maneuvered in to pick them up, the divers trade positions, and the second team then dives. Live boating is a technique that should only be performed by highly experienced divers and boat handlers. There is a high risk for accidents in live boating if the procedure is not followed properly.

Electric shock can also be a hazard when you dive on offshore oil platforms. Since these platforms are made from steel, they must have cathodic protection to help prevent the steel from corroding away in salt water. To help avoid problems, these platforms are covered with zinc anodes. However, on some platforms they may introduce live electrical current directly into the water. For this reason, you must be very careful when diving around any cables that are underwater on these structures.

Suction pipes are another potential hazard on offshore oil structures. Oil platforms are normally covered with machinery and diesel engines. In some cases, sea water is pumped aboard the platform for engine cooling, as ballast for floating structures, and for desalination (to create fresh water from sea water). Any suction pipe on an offshore structure will not usually be large

You must exercise extreme caution when diving on or around an oil rig. It is easy for a large fish to become entangled on these structures and there are numerous hazards that you must avoid.
(©Jesse Cancelmo. All rights reserved.)

enough to suck your body inside, but you could be trapped underwater if there is sufficient pull. Beware of any open pipes or gratings where there is obvious water flow.

It is not uncommon for workers aboard offshore platforms to fish during their free hours, nor is it uncommon for them to lose fish, lures, hooks, and other tackle. In addition, private fishing boats will frequently fish around these structures, too, and these fishermen will also lose gear. For these reasons, you can expect to find large amounts of monofilament line on almost any platform that is close to the coast. It is also not uncommon to find stainless steel wire hanging down from one level to the next of an offshore structure.

It is essential to have a sharp knife to free yourself if you become entangled with monofilament while underwater. A pair of side cutters or wire cutters must also be part of your equipment whenever you dive this type of structure. It's probably a good idea to attach the sidecutters to your buoyancy compensator with a short length of rope to help avoid losing it.

Falling objects are another hazard that can endanger you if you dive offshore platforms on a regular basis. Falling objects can vary in size from a pipe wrench accidentally dropped over the side to a 50 foot length of pipe. Obviously, a large falling object can definitely ruin your day and you must constantly be on the alert for this type of hazard. If you hear something falling through the structure, pay attention and be prepared to move out of the way.

If you spear a large fish on a remote offshore platform, there is always the potential that the fish will go deep or head for open water. It is also possible for a fish to become hopelessly entangled in the structure. In these situations you must be prepared to cut the fish free if necessary.

GET TO KNOW EACH DIVE SITE INTIMATELY

The most successful spearfishermen get to know each dive site intimately by returning to the site over and over again. They know where the fish will be at a given site and what time of year they will be there. They recognize changes in the site and how it will affect the fish.

Many spearfishermen find that drawing a map of the site will help them to learn it. The drawing should be updated as conditions at the site change. The drawing should include terrain features, such as sand and rocks, kelp, wrecks, and any unusual hazards. The drawing need not be a work of art; even a sketch will be very useful. Keep these sketches with your dive logs, but don't let your dive buddy see them!

CHAPTER 6

TYPES OF FISH

There are thousands of different types of fish found in the oceans and fresh water, but there are probably less than a few hundred fish that are considered good to eat <u>and</u> can be taken by spearfishing. If you want to be a successful, conservation minded spearfisherman, you must be able to properly identify the fish you intend to hunt and know that species' habits. This can be more difficult than it sounds because some species of fish may be very similar in appearance to other species, yet the regulations pertaining to each fish may be very different.

As you might expect, different types of fish are found in different habitats. You wouldn't expect to find a large, pelagic fish (open ocean) fish like a wahoo on a shallow water rock reef. The more you know about what a fish eats, when it breeds, and where it likes to hide, the more likely you will be to get the fish you want. It is probably more important to know where to find fish than to know how to shoot them. Learning to shoot fish is relatively easy compared to learning how and where to find them.

This chapter will provide a brief overview of the more popular fish taken by spearfishermen in the U.S. and Caribbean waters. In the bibliography in the back of the book you will find a listing of some of the better fish identification books that should be part of your diving library.

This chapter is organized by broad categories known as the "family" of fish. It should only be considered an introduction to the more popular and common fish that divers take while spearfishing. I have not included the larger game fish, such as tuna, that are only taken by highly experienced bluewater hunters.

A Bit About Scientific Names

To avoid confusion, I have listed the common name for each fish as well as the scientific name. The same fish may go by a variety of common names, but each species will have only one scientific name. The scientific names are in Latin and they are italicized.

The problem with common names is that the same fish may go by different names in different parts of the country. Conversely, entirely different fish may also be called by the same name; where one may be good to eat while the other is considered "trash".

If you want to be truly knowledgeable about fish and you intend to read the scientific literature, it will be essential to know the scientific name as well as the common name. See the appendix in the back of the book for a complete explanation about scientific names.

In most cases, you will only need to know the genus and species names of a particular fish to look it up in any scientific text. In many cases, fishing laws are written around particular species of fish, so it is important to be able to properly identify the correct fish that is referred to in the law.

It is your legal responsibility to be able to correctly identify the fish in your possession. Just as ignorance of the law is not considered a valid excuse in court, your inability to correctly identify the fish you have taken will not get you off the hook if you are ticketed by a game warden.

> WARNING: Be sure to check the fishing laws for your state each year. Species, size, and catch regulations change on a regular basis. Fish that may be legal to take one year may be banned from sport take the next. Know your local regulations and heed them carefully.

Freshwater Fish
Family - Cyprinidae
Common Carp

Of all the freshwater fish, the common carp, (*Cyprinus carpio*), is the fish that may be most frequently legally hunted in fresh water. Carp were first introduced into the United States in 1831

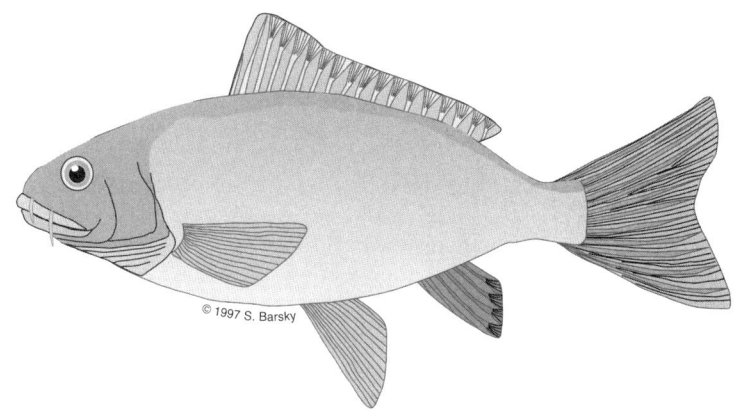

The common carp is widely distributed throughout freshwater lakes in the U.S.

and as such are referred to by biologists as an "introduced species" or a "non-native species". Since introduced species usually "out-compete" native species, biologists generally consider them to be pests and because of this they may be freely hunted.

Carp start life fairly gray in color but change as they age to a brassy, green color. They grow to a maximum length of 48 inches and up to 65 pounds.

Carp can survive under very adverse conditions and may be found in very turbid water. They are widely distributed in fresh water throughout the United States. Carp can be approached by both scuba and skin divers.

SALTWATER FISH
FAMILY GADIDAE
ATLANTIC COD

Cod (*Gadus morhua*) is a popular food and game fish. They are found from Southern Greenland to Cape Hatteras on the east coast.

Although their body color may vary widely, many of these fish are brown with reddish spots. They have a distinct lateral line down their sides and a barbel that hangs down from their lower jaw.

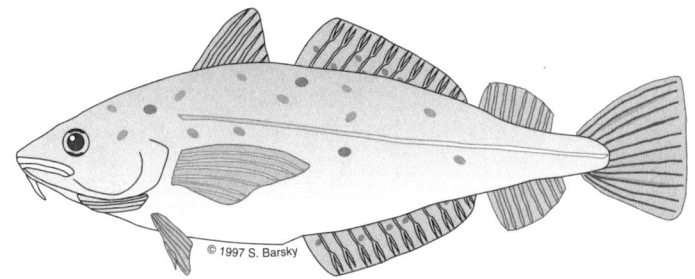

Cod are a common fish that may be taken by the scuba diver.

Cod prefer rough bottom terrain, i.e., rocky bottoms or areas of sand and rock, and are frequently found on or around shipwrecks. They are found at virtually all diving depths. They feed on small fish, crustaceans, mollusks, and worms, so wherever these animals are common you can expect to find cod.

Cod are typically schooling fish and they migrate during the spring spawning season to areas where the water temperature is between 39 and 43 degrees F. They are frequently taken by scuba diving spearfishermen.

FAMILY - BOTHIDAE
CALIFORNIA HALIBUT

Halibut are one of the most popular fish for spearfishermen to land on the west coast. These fish can get quite large and are excellent eating. The largest halibut are usually the females.

California halibut (*Paralicthys californicus*) may be taken year round, although they are taken in greater numbers during the late spring and early summer months. During this period, they tend to come into shallow water. If you find one fish, there are usually others close by. Stay alert once you've spotted the first halibut of the day.

Halibut may also be frequently found near the mouth of rivers, streams, and estuaries. Be sure to consult local fishing regulations because some states have restrictions on spearfishing in these areas. They are normally found on sandy bottoms, although I have seen halibut lying on the deck of a shipwreck and on rocky reefs, but these are exceptions rather than the norm.

The range of the California halibut is from the Quillayute River in Washington to Magdalena Bay in Baja California, Mexico. The largest fish grow to 60 inches and 72 pounds, but it is rare to see a fish over 40 pounds. In California, the largest fish are generally found at the Channel Islands while smaller fish are found along the coast. The fish on the coast also tend to be more "skittish" and will bolt at the first sign of a diver. However, I have seen halibut that thought they were camouflaged and did not move even when I have swam up right next to them.

Skip Dunham took this California halibut at Santa Cruz Island.

Halibut are ambush feeders; i.e., they tend to lie on the bottom and wait for prey to swim by, rather than actively swimming and hunting. When they see their prey, they "erupt" off the bottom to capture their food. They will feed on anchovies, sardines, squid, and other small fish.

Probably the ideal place to spear a halibut is just behind the gill plates, along the spine. A good spinal shot can totally disable even a large fish. Unless you have an exceptionally powerful gun you will probably not get good penetration anywhere around the head on a big fish. In addition, the head is a small target and easily missed.

Halibut have small, sharp teeth and can deliver a nasty bite if they manage to get hold of you. To subdue a speared halibut, some divers will reach under their gill plate and rip out their gills. This is a very effective technique for overpowering an active fish. However, you must wear thick gloves to do this since their gill rakers are extremely sharp and can produce a nasty cut by themselves.

SUMMER FLOUNDER

Summer flounder (*Paralicthys dentatus*) is an east coast fish that is closely related to the California halibut, belonging to the same family and genus. They are found from Maine to South Carolina.

Summer flounder has an appearance that is quite similar to the California halibut, but their bodies are a bit broader. These fish grow up to a length of 37 inches and a weight of 26 pounds. They are found on sandy or muddy bottoms. They may mimic the color of the bottom and bury themselves so that only their eyes are visible, although you will usually be able to see the outline of their body.

These fish feed on the bottom as well as in mid-water. Their preferred diet includes squid, worms, and crustaceans.

During the summer months these fish move into shallow water and can be found in estuaries and creeks, as well as near piers and bridges. During the winter months they move out into deeper water.

Flounder, like halibut, move with the tides and will move inshore to feed during a high tide. These fish are frequently taken by scuba divers.

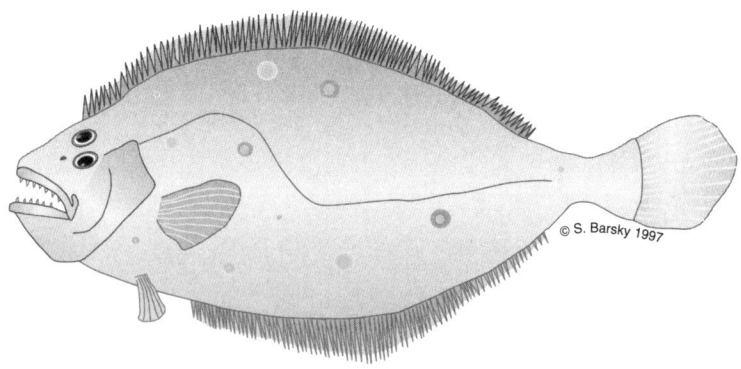

Summer flounder are closely related to the California halibut and have a similar appearance.

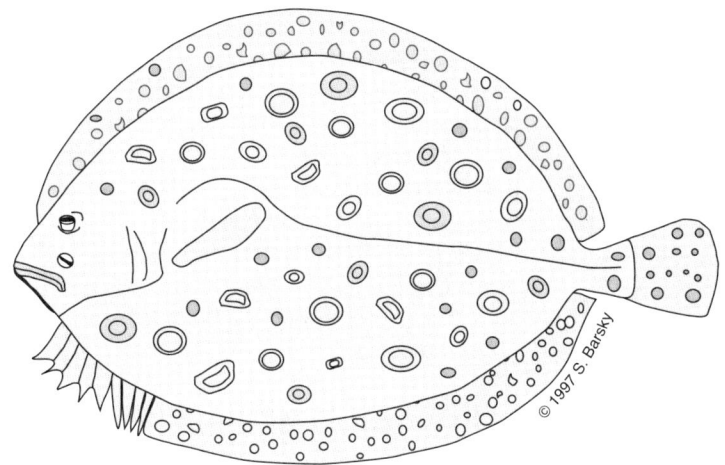

Peacock flounder are a popular species to hunt in Florida.

PEACOCK FLOUNDER

The peacock flounder (*Bothus lunatus*) is found from Florida to Brazil. These fish are primarily brown with bright blue rings on their bodies and blue spots on their heads and fins. They grow to maximum size of 18 inches and most fish speared in Florida range between two and six pounds. Like the California halibut and the summer flounder, these are considered "lefteye flounders", i.e., both their eyes are on the left side of their head.

Peacock flounders prefer warm, clear water. In the spring in the Panama City area of Florida, these fish will move into shallow water when the temperature warms up to 62 degrees F. They will normally remain in shallow water for about five or six weeks and once the water becomes much warmer they move back out into the Gulf. They move back inshore when the water cools down a bit in the fall to spawn, and then move offshore again as the water becomes colder.

Like the California halibut, peacock flounders tend to remain relatively close together when they are lying on the bottom. If you see one fish, look carefully around for the next one.

Peacock flounders feed on anchovies. When you see a cloud of anchovies milling around close to a wreck, look closely because it is likely these flounders will be lying beneath them, waiting for the opportunity to feed.

Rather than use a speargun, some spearfishermen along Florida's gulf coast use a three to four foot long 3/8 inch diameter stainless rod to hunt for peacock flounder. One end of the rod is sharpened and a hole is drilled in the other end through which a nylon line is threaded and tied off. The end of the line is knotted or in some way blocked. The entire arrangement resembles a giant sewing needle and thread. Once a fish is speared it is slid up the shaft onto the line, followed by the next fish, until enough fish have been obtained for a meal.

FAMILY PERCICTHYIDAE (TEMPERATE BASSES)
STRIPED BASS

The striped bass *(Morone saxatalis)* is a popular east coast fish. They range from the St. Lawrence river in the north to the St. Johns river in Florida. Along the Gulf Coast they can be found from western Florida to Louisiana.

On the west coast, striped bass are found from central California to southern Oregon, although they are rarely hunted here. They are also found in freshwater lakes and rivers in more than 30 states. Striped bass migrate and tend to move north during the spring and summer months, and south in the fall. They are a schooling fish.

Striped bass are opportunistic predators, but feed primarily on other fish. They may move into very shallow water to feed. Although striped bass can grow as large as six feet in length and

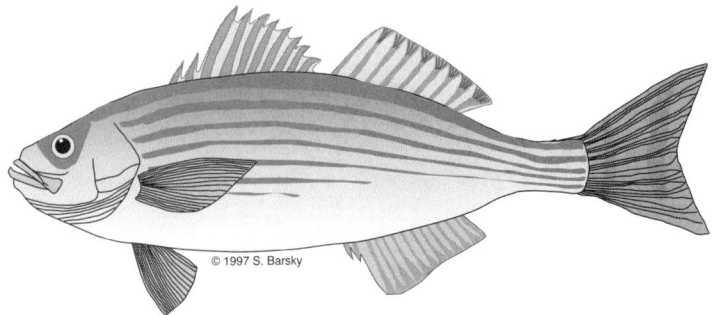

Striped bass can be found in both fresh and salt water, along both coasts of the U.S.

125 pounds, they are rarely more than 50 pounds. They are an excellent eating fish.

Like salmon, striped bass have the unusual capacity to survive in both salt and fresh water. This places them in a special category known as anadromous fishes.

You may also hear striped bass referred to as "stripers", "rockfish", and "squid hounds".

FAMILY RACHYCENTRIDAE
COBIA

Cobia (*Rachycentron canadum*) are a unique fish in that they are the only species in their family, i.e., the cobia themselves. They are found on the east coast of the U.S., from Massachusetts south to Argentina, but may be found in warm seas around the world. They are considered a trophy fish for any spearfisherman.

Cobia can often be found near sea buoys or other floating structures, as well as on or near shipwrecks. They are taken both in shallow coastal waters as well as in the open sea. They feed primarily on squid, shrimp, and crabs.

Cobia are large, powerful fish that may grow as big as 150 pounds, but are more commonly seen in the 10-50 pound range. Their maximum length can get up to six feet. They tend to travel in small schools of four to ten fish and may accompany sharks or rays. If you see a ray or a shark but don't see a cobia directly accompanying it, keep your eyes open. It is likely there may be a cobia along momentarily.

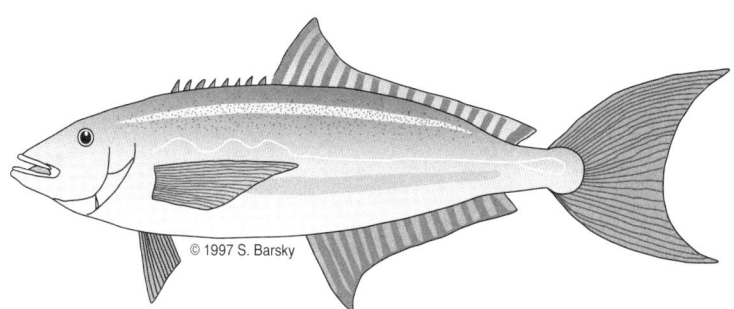

Cobia can grow to a weight of up to 150 pounds, although smaller fish are much more common.

Types of Fish

When a cobia sees you underwater they will frequently swim right up to you to check you out. This is your time to shoot. If you fail to get off a shot during their initial approach you probably won't get a second chance.

Although the flesh of a cobia is quite firm, it is important to get complete penetration with your shaft or you risk losing the fish. Your gun should have enough power to put the shaft all the way through their body. It's also essential to be sure the fish is dead before you bring it aboard your boat because a live fish can do tremendous damage aboard.

Cobia are generally considered to be an excellent eating fish.

FAMILY SERRANIDAE (SEA BASSES)
CALICO BASS (KELP BASS)

Calico bass (*Paralabrax clathratus*), also known as kelp bass, are a good eating fish and one of the most popular to hunt on the west coast. They are most commonly found from northern California to southern Baja, Mexico.

Calico bass are extremely wary fish and you must be very stealthy to consistently land the larger ones. They are found in kelp forests and in holes and crevices in the rock reefs. Use your flashlight to look in holes for these fish.

If there is a thermocline at depth they will usually be found in the warmer water above it. Their preferred depth range is from just below the surface to 70 feet, although they have been seen as deep as 150 feet. It is diffi-

Mark Perlstein shot these calico bass at Anacapa Island near Ventura, California.

cult to approach these fish much closer than six feet.

Calico bass have large eyes and their bodies are normally greenish or brownish gray with darker mottling on their sides. Their lower bodies are normally a yellowish silver. These fish rarely grow larger than 20 inches in length with a maximum weight of 12 pounds.

BLACK SEA BASS (OR GIANT SEA BASS)

For many years, California free divers hunted black sea bass (*Stereolepis gigas*) and pictures of them appeared in all the popular diving magazines up until the late 60's. The fish were on the verge of extinction when the California Department of Fish and Game made it illegal to land them in California waters. Today they appear to be making a good comeback and there are now resident populations at Anacapa, Santa Cruz, Santa Barbara and San Clemente islands and along the Palos Verdes Peninsula.

Black sea bass may still be taken in Mexico. They are a popular target for traveling underwater hunters. They are found in depths from 18 to 100 feet of water. They are commonly found in kelp forests and on rocky reefs.

Juvenile black sea bass are bright red with black spots, but the adults are gray with black spots on their side.

While black sea bass may be legally taken in Mexico, they are a protected species in California.

The range of the black sea bass is from the Gulf of California in Mexico to Humboldt Bay in California. They grow in size up to seven feet in length and 557 pounds. They are not a difficult fish to spear and can be easily approached, but you must have the proper gear to land a large fish. Most experienced divers will not shoot a black sea bass, even where it is legal to take them.

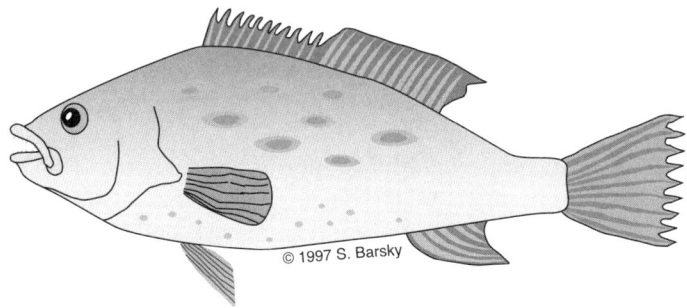

Broomtail grouper are another protected species in California.

BROOMTAIL GROUPER

Broomtail grouper (*Mycteroperca xenarcha*) are another fish that may be hunted in Mexico but not in the state of California. Their range is from Paita, Peru to San Francisco Bay, although they are rarely seen in California waters.

Broomtail groupers are found at depths down to 70 feet. The largest recorded individual caught weighed 97 pounds. These fish are normally gray, but may have brown and green mottling.

NASSAU GROUPER

The Nassau grouper (*Ephiephelus striatus*) is just one of a number of groupers that is found on the east coast off North Carolina down to Bermuda, and in the Gulf of Mexico. It grows up to four feet in length and to a maximum weight of 55 pounds.

Nassau groupers have four or five dark bars on the sides of their bodies and a "tuning fork" shaped pattern on their foreheads. They use this coloration to blend in with sea fans and other reef structure as they sit in ambush for other small fish to swim by. They can also be found feeding along the edge of drop-offs. Despite their normally lethargic manner, they are capable of rapid movement.

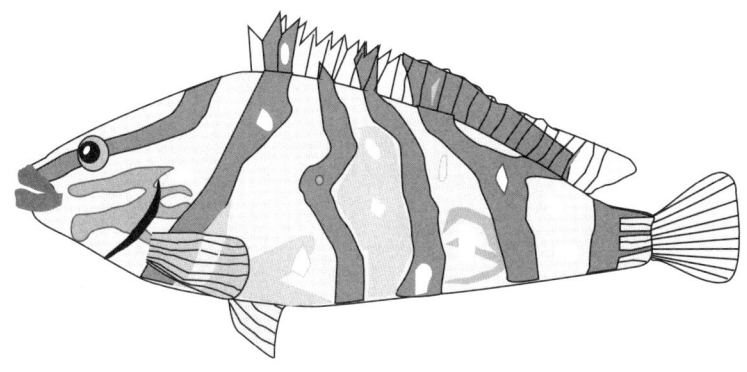

Nassau groupers are curious fish.

Nassau groupers are commonly found on coral reefs and in seagrass beds at depths down to 100 feet. They may frequently be seen at "cleaning stations", being relieved of parasites by bands of small gobies.

Always try to get a head shot on a grouper, if possible. A good shot will immediately paralyze or kill the fish and that's your goal.

One of the more curious fish on the reef, Nassau groupers will often follow divers for extended periods of time. They respond strongly, but cautiously to sound. When they breed, they gather together in large "spawning aggregations".

Nassau groupers are a good eating fish.

Family Hexagrammidae

Lingcod

Lingcod (*Ophiodon elongatus*) are another popular west coast fish that are found from Baja California, all the way to Alaska. They prefer colder, deeper waters, although under the right conditions they may be found just below the surface. These fish can get quite large, up to 41 pounds in California and up to 105 pounds in the colder waters of British Columbia. Lings are quite abundant from northern California through Oregon and make up a substantial portion of the recreational catch taken by divers and fishermen.

While lingcod often have greenish flesh when first cleaned, the color of the meat is white once it is cooked. Skip Dunham speared these two fish off Santa Rosa Island.
(© Jim Finch. All rights reserved.)

Lingcod are easy fish to spear. Most of the time they can be found lying around, motionless, on rocks, although they can also be found on sandy bottoms, and in eel grass beds. They normally will not make any attempt to swim away as you approach.

Lings have very rough gill rakers, so if you put your hand inside them be sure that you are wearing gloves. They have a large mouth relative to their size and sharp, but rather short teeth.

Lingcod feed on other fish, squid, and octopus. Their color varies from gray-brown to green. Even their flesh occasionally has a greenish tinge, but this disappears when the fish is cooked.

CABEZON

Cabezon (*Scorpaenicthys marmoratus*) are an unusual fish in that they have no scales on their bodies. They feed primarily on squid, octopus, and abalone.

Cabezon are readily taken by scuba divers all along the west coast of the U.S.

Like lingcod, cabezon can be frequently found lying on the bottom, particularly on rock reefs, oil platforms, and wrecks. They can get rather large, and grow up to 39 inches in length.

Cabezon are found along the entire length of the U.S. west coast up to Sitka, Alaska, and down to Pt. Abreojos in Baja California. They are commonly seen at diving depths and as deep as 250 feet.

Cabezon actually lay their eggs in a "nest" and the males guard the eggs until they hatch. Good sportsmanship demands that you avoid shooting a male guarding a nest to give the his offspring a chance to survive.

Cabezon may be reddish (primarily males) or greenish (primarily females) in color with vivid dark and light mottling. They have large eyes and sharp spines on their dorsal and caudal fins. Like lingcod, their flesh is colored, but it's blue instead of green. The color disappears when the fish is cooked.

The roe of a cabezon is extremely poisonous and consuming them can make you quite sick. Never eat the eggs of this fish.

FAMILY CORYPHAENIDAE
DOLPHIN

Dolphin (*Coryphaena hippurus*) are also referred to as dorado or "mahi-mahi". Dolphin are in no way related to the air breathing mammals, like "Flipper®". They are found in all tropical and temperate seas.

Dolphin have a large blunt head with small eyes. They have a single long dorsal fin and a broad tail fin. They are beautifully

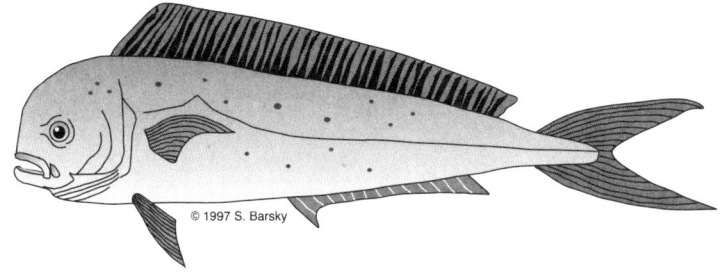

Dolphinfish are also known as "mahi mahi".

colored an iridescent yellowish green with blue spots and go through vivid color changes after they are speared and before they die. Once they are dead their coloration rapidly fades.

Dolphin are found around the world in warm seas. They are primarily an open ocean fish and will hang out under floating mats of seaweed in water no colder than 68 degrees F. They are extremely fast swimmers and are curious fish. While they are commonly found in large schools, solitary fish may also be seen. They feed on fish, squid, and crustaceans (crabs, shrimp, etc.).

It is rare for a scuba diver to see a dolphin and they are hunted almost exclusively by freedivers. They are an excellent eating fish.

Family Scorpaenidae
Rockfish

There are numerous species of rockfish (genus *Sebastes*) and telling them apart can be a challenge for even a trained marine biologist. As their name implies, rockfish are usually found on rocky reefs. They are good eating.

Rockfish are characterized by large eyes, distinctive coloration, and a high, spiny dorsal fin. Their coloration can range from black to yellow to bright red, depending upon the species. They are not particularly fast swimmers, when compared to pelagic (open ocean) fishes.

There are numerous species of rockfish along the west coast that are taken by divers, but only a few deep water species are found on the east coast.

Rockfish are not very large fish and it is unusual to find any individuals of most species over sixteen inches in length. They feed primarily on small juvenile fish, crabs, and shrimp.

Some of the more popular west coast rockfish include the vermillion rockfish, grass rockfish, kelp rockfish, and the gopher rockfish. Some west coast species, like the copper rockfish, may range from Alaska to Baja, while others, like the black-and-yellow rockfish have a much narrower range that only extends from Eureka, California to Baja. There are only a few species of rockfish on the east coast and these fish are primarily taken in deep water by commercial trawlers.

Rockfish aren't particularly large fish. For example, the grass rockfish grows to a maximum length of only 22 inches, while the gopher rockfish only reaches 15.5 inches.

FAMILY LABRIDAE (WRASSES)
TAUTOG

Tautog (*Tautoga onitis*) is a popular fish species found on the east coast of the U.S. Like the California sheephead, they are one of the few species of fish where the male and female animals are distinctly different.

Male tautogs are dark olive to dark gray with a white chin and a white blotch on the side. Female tautogs are mottled and blotched with a darker gray to black on a pale olive, brown, or

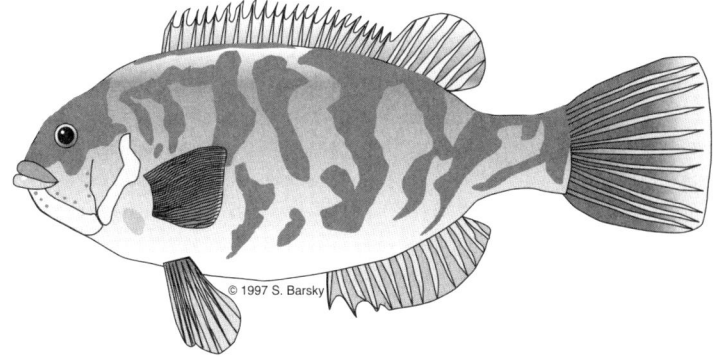

Tautog are readily taken by scuba divers on the east coast. This is the male of the species.

gray background. The dorsal and ventral fins and lips of the male are also much larger than those of the female.

Tautog are a shallow water fish and are found on rocky bottoms and around pilings, breakwaters, and wrecks. While you may see several of these fish together at one time, they are not a schooling fish. They feed primarily on mollusks (clams, oysters, etc.) and crustaceans.

Their range is from Nova Scotia to South Carolina, although they are most abundant from Cape Cod to Delaware Bay. Between May and October these fish gather in bays and estuaries to spawn. They prefer water temperatures between 46 and 71 degrees F, and temperature plays a major role in their movements.

Larger tautog grow up to three feet in length and weigh up to 22 pounds. This is a fish that is readily taken by scuba divers.

CALIFORNIA SHEEPHEAD

The wrasses are all included in the family *Labridae*, which includes fish such as the California sheephead (*Semicossyphus pulcher*) and the tropical hogfish and tautog.

Along the west coast, the California sheephead is found from Cape San Lucas in Baja, Mexico to as far north as Monterey, California. They are commonly seen at sport diving depths. Sheephead grow to lengths of up to three feet and weigh up to 36 pounds. They are usually solitary fish, although they sometimes form small schools.

Skip Dunham proudly displays two large male sheephead.
(Photo © Pete Ryan. All rights reserved.)

The sheephead undergoes a sex change, from female to male, as they grow. Female sheephead are smaller and are a pale pink in color. Male sheephead are dramatically colored in red, black, and white.

Many scientists believe that this change is at least partially initiated by the number of males in a given area. If there are enough males, no females grow and change into a male. If the number of males is too low, the largest female becomes a male.

These fish are active only during daytime hours, sleeping in caves and crevices at night. They grow relatively slowly and a large fish may be over 50 years old!

Sheephead are not particularly smart fish, although they have become much more wary of divers than they were 20 years ago. In California, it is easy to lure them into shooting range by breaking up sea urchins, which is one of their favorite foods.

Sheephead are a tasty fish. They can be difficult to clean, but the flesh is soft and takes seasoning well. Boiled sheephead tastes somewhat like crab if placed in a sealed plastic bag and allowed to sit in the refrigerator for a day or two.

HOGFISH

Hogfish (*Lachnolaimus maximus*), also known as "hog snapper", are found in the Gulf of Mexico and Caribbean. Most do not exceed three feet in length and are commonly found at sport diving depths. They have large scales and are capable of rapid changes in the color of their bodies.

Look for hogfish feeding on sandy bottoms where they will orient themselves vertically in a head-down position, blowing the sand away to expose the buried animals on which they feed.

Hogfish can grow to be quite large and are good eating.

However, they may also be found on the reef itself. They are very active fish and swim almost constantly. They prefer warmer waters and will move with temperature changes.

Hogfish have been implicated in some cases of ciguaterra, a serious type of fish poisoning that can be fatal. Be sure to consult with local divers before spearing and eating hogfish, as fish poisoning occurs sporadically. In most cases, hogfish make good eating.

Ciguaterra occurs when a large fish such as a barracuda has been feeding on smaller fish that have fed on poison producing plankton. Eating the flesh of an affected fish causes the poisoning. Cooking the fish does not neutralize the poison.

Ciguaterra can be extremely serious and has been known to cause death. The initial symptoms include tingling of the lips, tongue and throat, followed by numbness. The victim may also suffer nausea, vomiting, and diarrhea. Victims usually become extremely weak and in severe cases the nervous system is dramatically affected.

Recovery from ciguaterra is slow. If you think you may be suffering from ciguaterra poisoning it is essential to seek immediate medical help.

In areas where there are no spearfishermen, hogfish can be easily approached. Wherever there is hunting however, they are much more wary and it can be difficult to get close to get a good shot.

Hogfish flesh is extremely delicate and if a fish is not killed immediately it will tear itself up to get off. Your best bet is a spine shot or head shot. Hogfish can be taken by both skin and scuba divers.

FAMILY BALISTIDAE
TRIGGERFISH

Triggerfish (*Balistes sp. - Note: the sp. means there are a number of different species in this genus*) are a popular type of fish to hunt along the east coast, in the Gulf of Mexico, and in Hawaii. There are numerous species of triggerfish including the gray triggerfish (*Balistes capriscus*) found on the east coast, and the queen triggerfish (*Balistes vetula*) common in the Caribbean.

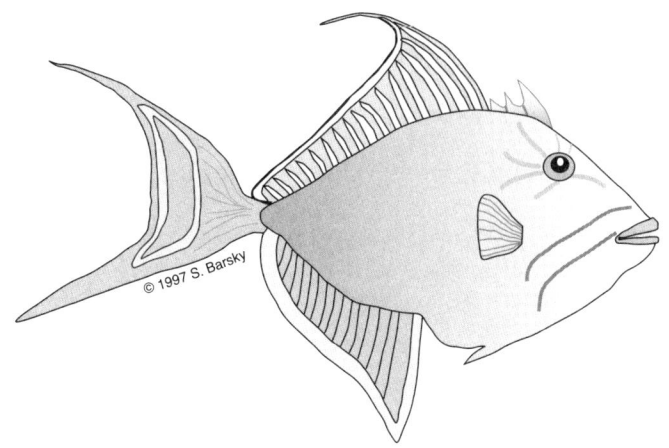

Triggerfish are frequently taken by scuba divers.

All triggerfish have a similar body shape and are extremely aggressive, curious fish. They have a tough, beak-like jaw and small sharp teeth. They have been known to frequently nip at divers and can definitely take small but painful bites from your hands, fingers, and ears. It's been said that if triggerfish grew as large as groupers there would probably be no such thing as scuba diving! Having been bitten by triggerfish on more than one occasion I would be inclined to agree...

Triggerfish get their name from the mechanism that controls their first dorsal spine. The small second spine behind the first one must be depressed or "triggered" before the first spine can be lowered. Triggerfish use the action of the first spine to wedge themselves in crevices in reefs to avoid predators.

Gray triggerfish do not get very large, with a maximum length of one foot, but Queen triggerfish may grow to double that size. Triggerfish are easily taken by scuba divers.

FAMILY SCIAENIDAE (CROAKERS)
WHITE SEABASS

White seabass (*Atractoscion nobilis*) are an excellent eating fish that are prized by spearfishermen along the entire west coast. They are found as far south as Magdalena Bay in Mexico all the way up to Juneau, Alaska.

White seabass are considered a prized species on the west coast. Matt Lum is acknowledged as one of the best underwater hunters when it comes to taking these fish.

White seabass are considered a great challenge by most spearfishermen because they are so elusive. Many dedicated spearfishermen have spent years hunting white seabass without success.

White seabass have very soft flesh so the choice of spear tip that you use is critical. Most experienced hunters prefer a slip tip that detaches easily from the shaft and has a wide surface area that makes it more difficult for the fish to pull it out. This is especially important if you don't put your tip all the way through the fish.

Although white seabass are generally considered an open water/bluewater fish, they are frequently taken in shallow, murky coves at the Channel Islands. They feed primarily on squid, anchovies, mackerel, and sardines.

Like most croakers, white seabass actually do make loud croaking noises underwater. Successful spearfishermen train themselves to listen for their sounds and can tell whether the fish are in the area or not.

White seabass tend to congregate together, in schools that can be quite large. If you see one fish it's usually a safe bet that there are more in the area.

FAMILY SPHYRAENIDAE (BARRACUDAS)
GREAT BARRACUDA

The great barracuda (*Sphyraena barracuda*) is an imposing fish with a mouth full of teeth. Although they look menacing, they

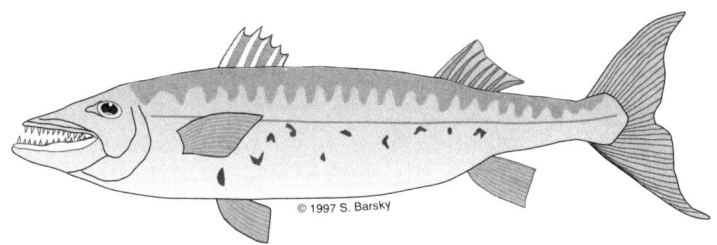

The great barracuda has been implicated in many cases of ciguaterra.

have rarely been known to attack humans. Like sharks, however, they are attracted by blood and may attack speared fish. They are among the fastest swimming fish in the sea.

Great barracuda may grow to a length of six feet and up to 106 pounds, although fish this large are rare. They are an extremely curious, inquisitive fish and may follow divers for hours underwater. For the new diver, their frequent jaw flexing, that helps them breathe by pumping water over their gills, may be a bit unnerving. They have been taken by both freedivers and scuba divers.

The great barracuda is capable of changing its coloration depending on where it is swimming. While adult fish tend to be solitary or congregate in small schools, the young barracuda will school with dozens of other individuals.

Never spear a barracuda unless you can be sure of a good shot. Their body is delicate and their flesh is soft. Unless you hit them in the head or spine there is a good chance that they will tear the spear out of their body. In addition, attempting to subdue a large, wounded, angry barracuda could be extremely hazardous to your health.

Barracuda seem to prefer water temperatures warmer than 60 degrees F. They get excited about anything thrashing in the water and will move in to investigate. If you are diving on a wreck, you can scrape some worms or other growth off the wreck to get the smaller fish to feed and the barracudas will move right in to check it out.

Although they look menacing, barracudas are not too smart and are an easy target in most cases. Even just banging on a wreck with your knife may attract barracuda as they are extremely curious fish. If you act like you are not interested in them, they will be more inclined to come close to you. Chasing a barracuda is only worthwhile if you need some exercise and don't really need a fish for dinner.

Barracuda are one of the most common sources of "ciguaterra poisoning" and the larger the fish, the more toxin it has in its body. There is no method for identifying which fish are carrying the toxin.

FAMILY CARANGIDAE (JACKS)
CALIFORNIA YELLOWTAIL

Yellowtail *(Seriola dorsalis)* are considered one of the best eating fish found along the West coast as far north as Washington and in the Gulf of California. They prefer warmer waters and are more common from Santa Barbara south. They are a challenging fish to hunt and spear, and are primarily landed by freedivers, although the exceptional scuba diver may have the chance to take one. They are closely related to the amberjacks that are found nearly worldwide in warm waters.

Yellowtail grow up to five feet in length and up to 80 pounds in weight. These are large, powerful fish that require a powerful gun. This is the type of fish that can take your gun and run away with it if you aren't properly equipped or don't get a good shot!

While the fins of a yellowtail are yellowish, they are not bright yellow as their name might imply. Their bodies are olive-

Matt Lum took this 64 pound yellowtail while diving off the dive boat Peace.
(© Nick Stobaugh. All rights reserved.)

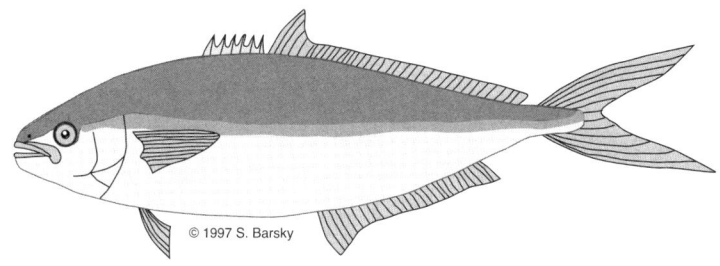

Yellowtail are skittish fish that are rarely seen or taken by scuba divers.

brown to brown in color, with a yellow stripe running down their side. They prefer water temperatures warmer than 63 degrees F.

Yellowtail are open water fish, although they can be found at the edge of deep water kelp beds, near offshore platforms, and along the fringes of rock reefs. Even though they are usually considered a "bluewater" fish they are not usually found below depths of 120 feet. They may frequently be found in open water, hanging out under drifting mats of kelp.

JACK CREVALLE (OR CREVALLE JACK)

Jack crevalle (*Caranx hippos*) are fast swimming fish found in warm water areas throughout North and South America. On the

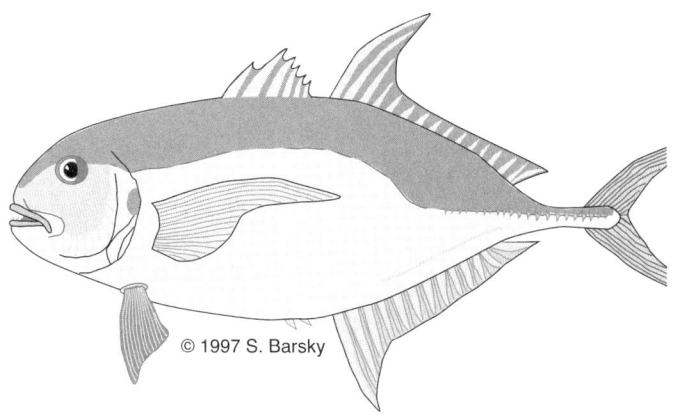

Jack crevalle can be approached by both skin and scuba divers.

Types of Fish

west coast they are found from San Diego south. They grow to a maximum length of five feet, but their weight does not generally exceed 20 pounds.

While the "dorsal" or back of these fish is generally greenish, the rest of their body tends towards a silvery appearance. Black blotches are found on their gill covers and pectoral fins.

Jack crevalle are usually found in open water and near "walls" where reefs drop off into deep water. They feed on fish, shrimp, and other invertebrates.

While jack crevalle are normally seen in schools, larger individuals may be solitary. They can be approached by both scuba and skin divers. They tend to be very curious and powerful fish.

Jack crevalle are not especially good eating fish. To help keep the meat fresh and tasty it's essential to bleed these fish if it will be more than a few hours before they are consumed.

AMBERJACK

There are several different species of amberjack (*Seriola sp.*) including the greater amberjack (*Seriola dumerili*) and the Pacific amberjack *(Seriola colburni).* All are large, fast swimming fish that are excellent eating.

On the east coast, the greater amberjack is found from Massachusetts to Brazil. Like the yellowtail, they are a schooling fish. Amberjacks can be found in both open water as well as on offshore reefs. The greater amberjacks grows to a size of up to 150 pounds. They are normally found at depths of 65 feet and deeper.

Consider yourself warned that amberjacks are tough, powerful fish. Never make the mistake of winding your speargun line

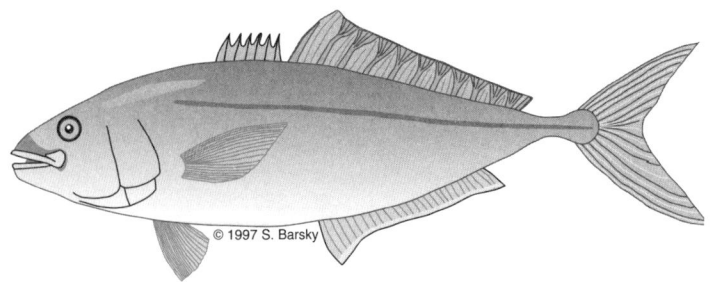

There are several species of amberjack, and all are good eating.

around your hand when attempting to subdue an amberjack. If the fish bolts, their pull on the line can cut your hand badly.

Be sure to subdue an amberjack before you bring it aboard your boat. Like any large fish, they could do a great deal of damage by thrashing about if they are not dead when brought aboard.

Amberjacks form small schools but adults may be solitary. They feed on fish and invertebrates. If they are schooling, once one or two fish have been shot they will move away from you.

Amberjacks have been known to cause ciguaterra poisoning. Be sure to check with local authorities before hunting amberjack to see if fish poisoning occurs in your area.

FAMILY SCOMBRIDAE
WAHOO

Wahoo (*Acanthocybium solanderi*) are also known as kingfish, ono, and jack mackerel in various parts of the U.S. In Hawaii, ono means "delicious" or "sweet" depending on who you talk to, and this is one of the most delicious fish you will ever taste.

Wahoo grow very large, up to 83 inches long and 183 pounds. They have a slender, long body with long jaws and many teeth. They have what is known as "counter-shading"; i.e., a dark upper body that is blue in color and a lighter underbelly that is almost white. They have a series of dark, distinct vertical bars along their sides.

Countershading tends to help camouflage these fish from predators as well as making them more invisible to their prey. It makes it difficult for a fish to see them from above, as they blend in with the dark blue waters of the deep ocean. When they are

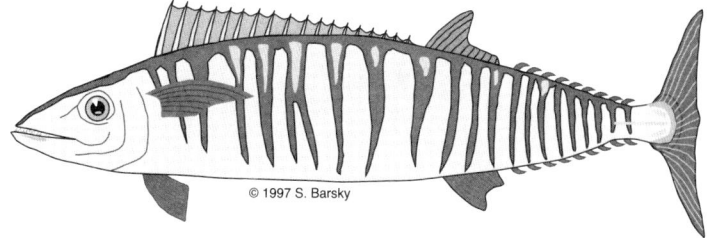

Wahoo are also known as "ono" in Hawaii.

viewed from below their white underbelly helps them to blend in with the bright sunshine above.

Wahoo are found worldwide in warm waters. In the U.S. they are found from New Jersey south on the east coast, in the Gulf of Mexico, and in Hawaiian waters. They are a fast swimming fish found in open water and are normally taken by free diving rather than with scuba.

Transporting and Cleaning Your Fish

There is nothing more pathetic than a spearfisherman who goes to the effort to spear a large fish and then handles his catch improperly so it is spoiled by the time he gets home from diving. Take the time to learn how to clean and transport your fish properly to get the maximum enjoyment from your prize.

Most fish should be gutted and bled out as soon as they are subdued and brought aboard the boat. Both of these actions will help to prevent the growth of bacteria in and on the fish. Bacteria is what causes fish to spoil and subsequently smell bad. Freshly cleaned fish should have only the mildest odor, if any at all.

To gut the fish, use a sharp knife and open the body cavity along the belly from the anal opening to the gills. Remove all of the internal organs and any blood that may flow as a result. Rinse the body cavity out thoroughly with fresh or salt water. It is not essential to remove the head and in some cases this may expose the flesh to bacterial contamination.

To bleed a fish, use a sharp knife and cut up inside the body cavity behind the head. On most fish you will find the large blood vessel that connects the rest of the body to the gills at the base of

Get your fish on ice as soon as possible.

the head. Be sure to allow all the blood to flow out before storing your fish for travel. If you bleed your fish and plan to get back in the water, you should move to another spot further up current before you dive again. Fish blood in the water will frequently attract sharks and they will follow the blood to its source.

Place the fish on ice as soon as possible. The cooler you can keep the fish, without freezing it, the better. If you don't have ice, but the water is cold, you can hang the fish in the water, although you should place it in a goody bag to help prevent it from being eaten by other fish. Some boats have free flooding fish boxes that also provide good storage for fish.

There is no need to fillet your fish until you get home and in some places it is illegal to fillet a fish until after it has been landed and measured by local fish and game authorities. Some states will allow you to fillet the fish as long as the fillets are a certain size and a patch of the fish's skin is intact so that the species can be properly identified. Be sure to check and follow whatever procedures are proper for your local area.

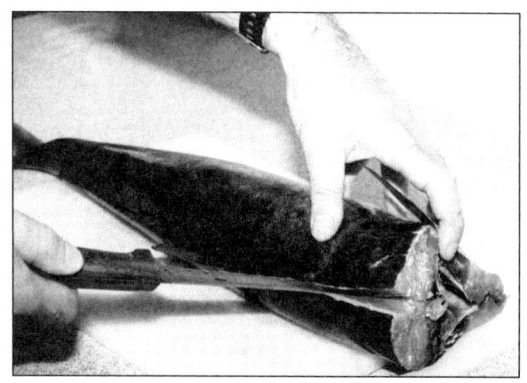
Learn how to properly filet and clean the fish that you intend to hunt.

There are different methods for filleting, cleaning, and preparing different species of fish. You need to learn how to clean the fish that you intend to hunt. Your best source of information on cleaning and filleting will be local spearfishermen.

Notes

CHAPTER 7

DEVELOPING YOUR SPEARFISHING TECHNIQUES

Spearfishing, like any form of hunting, requires that the hunter know his equipment intimately. Without a precise knowledge of the characteristics and capabilities of your gun it is unrealistic to expect that you can be a successful spearfisherman.

Spearguns are potentially lethal devices. You must develop safe habits for handling your speargun and treat it like any firearm. Although you will probably feel awkward handling your gun the first few times you take it out, it will quickly feel very natural. Just be sure that you take the time to think about how you are handling your gun initially and be methodical about your procedures. Spearfishing safety should become automatic to you in a short time.

LEARN TO ESTIMATE DISTANCES AND SIZES UNDERWATER

If you want to be a successful spearfisherman you must learn to estimate distances accurately underwater. You must know when a fish is at the limit or beyond the range of your gun. Shooting at a fish that is too far away is a useless exercise.

Another skill you must develop is the ability to look at a fish and know whether it is legal size or not. This can be quite difficult for the beginning spearfisherman. However, most states do not provide any allowances for a fish that is speared and is undersize. A short fish is still short, even if it "shrank" as you returned to the surface. In fact, it's amazing how much a fish will shrink by the time you get it up on the boat.

Many divers paint measuring lines on their gun or polespear, or apply waterproof tape to their weapon to provide measurements. This is a wise idea because without it you have no way of knowing for certain whether a fish is legal or not. Carrying a measuring tape with you underwater is an impractical solution to this problem.

In order to preserve our marine resources and to avoid getting a citation for a fishing violation, never shoot fish that are borderline legal. It's not worth the risk or embarrassment.

Importance of Practice

If you are a novice spearfisherman, it is important to get the feel of your gun and its power. You need to get in the water and learn how your gun behaves.

Just as a deer or bird hunter practices with his rifle or shotgun, you need to practice with your speargun. Before you attempt to shoot a fish for the first time you should practice on a target.

You can make targets out of plastic foam, or a wooden or metal frame with cloth or netting wrapped around it. Plastic foam is acceptable provided you don't use Styrofoam that breaks up into small pieces. Cut the material or make a frame in the shape of a fish and tie it to a lead diving weight so it floats a few feet off the bottom. Try shooting at the target from different angles.

Once you start spearfishing in the ocean, begin by hunting small, but legal size fish. It's unrealistic to think that you can go out and learn to hunt by targeting on large fish. Learn how your gun behaves and how to effectively stalk smaller fish. Once you have achieved a good success rate with smaller fish, you will be ready to move on to larger animals.

The Importance of Tides

Time your hunting according to the tides and you will usually find more fish. This is especially true for nearshore fish such as flounder, as opposed to deep water fish such as dolphin.

Some fish are more likely to be found during an incoming tide or at high tide, while others respond more strongly to a low tide or outgoing tide. This response to the state of the tide usually

Keep a copy of the tide tables handy and learn how the tides relate to the type of fish you hunt.

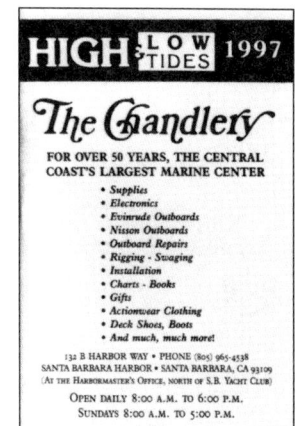

has more to do with the availability of food, although visibility may also be a factor.

Directly related to the tide is the state of the moon. In California, a small bait fish known as the grunion congregate to breed on certain sandy beaches after a full moon. Halibut feed on grunion and once they have fed are sluggish and less likely to bolt when they see a diver.

Most chandleries and many dive stores give away free sets of tide tables and tidal listings can also be found in most coastal newspapers. There are even inexpensive fishing watches that are available today that calculate the tides and indicate when fishing will be the most productive.

LOOK FOR TRANSITION ZONES

Whenever there is a transition zone between different types of underwater terrain you will usually have a productive area to find fish. For example, the edge of a rock reef where it meets the sand is usually good. Likewise, where coral reefs form "walls", and there are deep drop-offs, are areas that are rich in marine life.

What happens at a transition zone is that you have the meeting of different types of animals that tend to feed on

Drop-offs, where the reef falls away to deep water, are places where pelagic fish frequently come in to feed.

Look for transition zones, for example where the reef ends and the sand bottom begins.

each other. Larger pelagic (open ocean) fish will often come to the edge of a drop-off to feed. Halibut will often be found at the edge of a reef. Work these areas carefully and you will usually be rewarded with a successful hunt.

COVERING TERRITORY

One of the main keys to being a successful underwater hunter is to cover lots of territory, particularly if you are not seeing fish in the immediate area. Don't expect to jump over the side of the boat and sit on the bottom and have the fish come to you. The more habitat you see, the more fish you will probably encounter.

Of course, once you get into an area where you see fish, slow down and look carefully. The ocean has "live" areas and "dead" areas that change day by day and sometimes minute by minute. If an area "feels" right, but there are no fish on a particular day, it's worth noting in your log book for a return visit in the future.

It is particularly important to cover lots of ground if you are diving from a boat where there are numerous other divers. The further away you can get from the boat and everyone else, the better chance you will usually have of seeing more fish.

You should also make a real effort to get off the boat first, ahead of as many other people as possible. Most divers make noise that scare fish and drive them away from the area. By getting in the water first, when there has been less activity, you are more likely to see fish.

If you are diving from the beach, walk further down the beach than anyone else and get away from the crowds. Try to go to spots where the fewest people have been. There will usually be

You must cover lots of bottom in order to find fish.

more game there and the fish will be less spooky if they haven't had divers hunting them.

STALKING FISH

No matter which fins you own, no matter how fast you swim, you will never be able to swim faster than a large, healthy fish. This means that to land a fish, you must be smarter than the fish, which for some of us may not be all that easy...

Points of land that stick out from shore tend to be good places to look for fish.

Developing Your Spearfishing Techniques

You've got to learn to know where to look for fish and anticipate how they will behave and which way they will go if they are spooked. Preferably, you want to put yourself in a position, or create a situation, where the fish will come to you. Trying to swim quickly after a fish to shoot it is a losing proposition in most cases.

Ideally, you want to approach a fish, or have the fish approach you, so that you are slightly above the fish, shooting at a downward angle. This accomplishes two things. First, it puts you in a position where you can make a good shot at the head or the spine. Secondly, your shaft is not fighting against gravity in addition to having to overcome the drag of the water. It is extremely difficult to get a good shot when you are below a fish.

One of the better places to hunt fish is where the land forms a "point". Points of land that stick out into the sea, whether along the mainland or on an island, are usually good places to look for fish. The currents that flow around exposed points are usually much stronger than those that flow in more protected coves or bays. Wherever you have more current, you usually have better visibility, so you can see the fish. In areas where there are currents there are more nutrients in the water, which provide food for plants and animals. These nutrients and plants attract small fish which attract larger fish, providing you with something to hunt.

In most situations, fish tend to orient themselves so that they are swimming into a current. For this reason, whenever you dive around a point or along a reef face swim up into the current and you will have a better shot at the fish. Starting your dive into the current is normally considered good diving practice. By beginning your dive into the current you can ride the current back to the boat or your entry point when you are more fatigued at the end of the dive.

If you are hunting for halibut or other flatfish in dirty water, stay as high off the bottom as possible while still maintaining the bottom in clear view. Cover as much ground as possible. Most flatfish tend to bury themselves and often only their eyes and the outline of their body beneath the sand may be visible. Concentrate on looking for the outline of these fish rather than the whole fish.

Use the terrain like a topside hunter uses a duck blind to hide yourself from fish.

LEARN TO USE THE TERRAIN

Whenever possible, use the underwater terrain around you to your advantage. Just as a duck hunter topside might use a duck blind to hide from his quarry, you can hide behind rocks or wreckage to conceal yourself from fish as they swim by. If you are diving on a pinnacle, away from shore, lay on top of the rocks and try to blend in with the bottom.

If there is kelp in the area, orient your body to the kelp. If the kelp is floating vertically in the water, hang in an upright position. If the kelp is streaming out in the current, lean with the kelp so that you appear to be part of it.

Some divers feel that a camouflage wetsuit gives them a distinct advantage to blend in with the background. For certain types of fish and certain types of terrain, such as a kelp bed, this can be quite effective.

TEMPERATURE

Most fish are quite temperature sensitive and you need to learn what type of temperature conditions appeal to the fish you want to hunt. Water masses of different temperatures tends to form layers in the ocean, or what we call thermoclines. These can play a large part in determining where you will find your fish in the water column.

For example, calico bass are usually found above the cold thermocline in warmer water. If there is a noticeable thermocline you would be wasting your time hunting for calicos in the thermocline or below it. The same thing holds true for halibut; in most cases they prefer warmer water and will stay above the thermocline.

In certain situations in the ocean you will find broad temperature bands of water with markedly different temperatures. Some game fish tend to congregate along these temperature "breaks". Knowledgeable sportsmen know which fish tend to favor these types of conditions and seek them out when they are hunting. Check out how the fish in your area respond to these conditions.

TAKE ADVANTAGE OF FEEDING AND BREEDING

Fish tend to congregate during periods of heavy feeding or breeding. Take advantage of this fact whenever possible.

For example, when the squid spawn on the west coast during the spring, many different types of fish will come into shallow water to feed on the thousands of squid as they mate. Almost every type of fish that you can think of likes squid and also will

Keep an eye on any bait (small fish) that are in the water, such as anchovies or sardines.

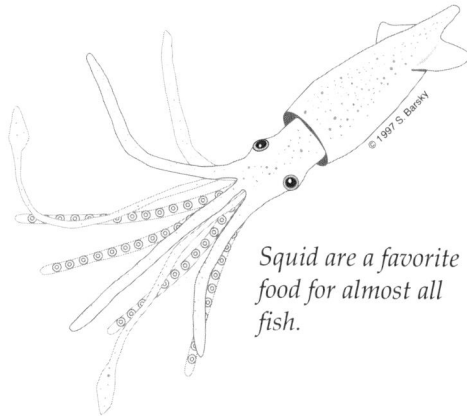

Squid are a favorite food for almost all fish.

show up to feed on these creatures. This is an excellent time to hunt.

If there are bait-fish in the water, you can be fairly certain that bigger fish are nearby. Keep an eye on the bait and monitor their behavior.

PLAY HARD TO GET

Just as in life where members of the opposite sex tend to be attracted to those individuals who ignore them or are otherwise unavailable, certain types of fish will respond better to divers who ignore their presence. By avoiding eye contact with some fish and actually swimming away from them they will be drawn to you to see what you are and what you are doing.

Use the fish's natural curiosity to make them come to you. Avoid aggressive behavior whenever possible because most fish are very attuned to this and will rapidly swim away from you.

With some fish, such as yellowtail, you may want to use a combination of these techniques. For example, Matt Lum sometimes follows a yellowtail until it speeds up to get away from him, then stops and waits. In many instances, the fish will turn around and swim back to check him out.

Certain species of fish are so curious they will act in ways that would seem to be a direct threat against their survival. Amberjack, which are a schooling fish, will almost always swim back in after you have shot one of the members of the school, to check out the

Rebreathers do not seem to give divers a dramatic edge in underwater hunting.

action. This will usually give you a shot at a second fish.

BE STEALTHY

Fish respond to noise, and while some fish are curious and may come to investigate a noise, many fish are frightened by noise and will run from it. In most instances, the quieter you can be and the more you can blend in with the environment, the better the chance you will have of seeing big fish. Fish are not totally dumb creatures, and big fish don't get to be big by being stupid.

For a scuba diver, being stealthy means streamlining your equipment as much as possible and avoiding dangling pieces of gear that may hit each other and create noise. For example, if your power inflator for your buoyancy compensator smacks against the buckles of your harness this will create noise that a fish can hear. Fasten your power inflator down in such a way that it doesn't flop around, yet is instantly accessible if you need it.

If you think about it, the mere act of adding air to your buoyancy compensator also produces noise. Of course, as a scuba diver there is no way to avoid producing bubbles which do scare many types of fish.

With the development of closed circuit and semi-closed circuit rebreathers there will certainly be some underwater hunters who will want to take advantage of this technology. The main benefit of this type of gear is that it gives off very little or no bubbles. Some people contend that using this type of gear for spearfishing is unsportsmanlike, that it gives the diver an unfair advantage.

My experiences with rebreather diving tells me that most underwater creatures still perceive you as a large, threatening animal that they will not allow to get close to them, despite the absence of bubbles from the rebreather. I would maintain that if you adopt a sportsmanlike attitude towards underwater hunting, using a rebreather is an acceptable diving method for spearfishing. However, the use of rebreathers for spearfishing is illegal in some states. Be sure to check local regulations before using this equipment for spearfishing.

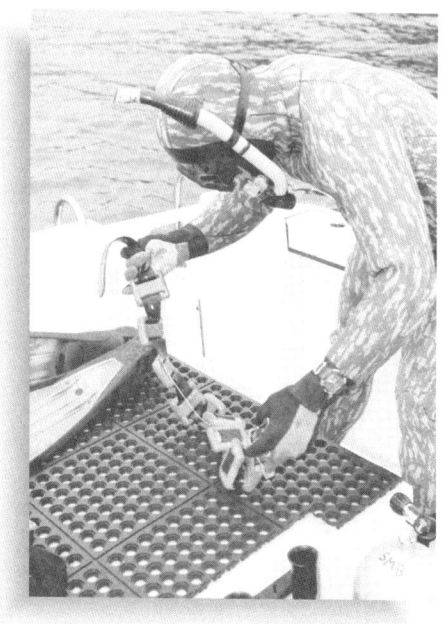

You must weight yourself properly for freediving.

Freediving allows you to be the most streamlined and potentially silent underwater hunter. You can generally swim faster as a freediver without the drag created by a buoyancy compensator, tank, and hoses.

Even freedivers can practice certain techniques that will help reduce the amount of noise they produce underwater. For example, if you keep your snorkel in your mouth when you submerge, the air that is in the snorkel will bubble out as you dive beneath the surface. However, if you drop the snorkel out of your mouth just before you submerge, the snorkel will be almost full of water before you even start your dive and will be less likely to make any noise as you slip beneath the waves.

Whether you are a freediver or a scuba diver it is important to start your dive as quietly as possible. Most divers splash, kick, and generally make a lot of noise as they leave the surface. This is exactly what you want to avoid doing if you want to be a successful underwater hunter.

A properly weighted scuba diver, who is weighted to make a precautionary decompression stop at the end of his dive, should be able to submerge by venting his buoyancy compensator. Scuba descents are normally made feet first, so there should be little need to splash about on the surface.

For freediving you should weight yourself so that you are positively buoyant by about two or three pounds on the surface, so that you don't need to kick to stay afloat. Once you submerge, the compression of your wetsuit will start and become greater the deeper you dive. Ideally, you want to be about one pound positive at a depth of twenty feet so that if you were to black out underwater on your way back up, you would still float up to the surface.

Keep in mind that as your wetsuit ages and the cells of the suit break down, your suit will be less buoyant. Similarly, if you gain or lose weight your buoyancy requirements will change. You must adjust your weighting over time for changes in the buoyancy of your suit as well as changes in your body.

Surface dives for freedivers must be performed so that the weight of your body drives you underwater. You should not start kicking until your fins are completely submerged. To do this without looking where your fins are means that you must develop a good sense of where your body is in the water. This is known as a "kinesthetic sense".

If you start kicking when your fins are still above the surface you will create a tremendous amount of noise and most of the fish that are nearby will leave the area at once. Try to slip beneath the surface as quietly as possible to minimize the amount of noise you make.

POSITION OF THE SUN

Pay attention to the position of the sun and how it affects your shadow on the bottom. If you are hunting bottom fish, such as flounder or halibut, you will want to avoid having your shadow cast ahead of you which would alert a fish to your presence. When strong shadows are present, be sure to approach these types of fish so that your shadow doesn't fall on the fish before you get in range.

Sea urchins are a ready source of "chum" that will attract fish.

(© 1997 Bob Evans/La Mer Bleu Productions)

CHUMMING

"Chumming" is one of the most effective means of attracting fish like California sheephead. To chum, you use some type of bait to attract fish to the area where you are hunting. The most common "bait" that is used is to break open sea urchins with your knife. The fish are attracted by the sea urchin eggs. You can also break open mussels or other shellfish.

The best technique for chumming is to move into an area, break open several large urchins, swim a distance away and repeat the procedure, then swim to another area and break open more urchins. After several minutes, return to the first area where you broke open urchins and there will be fish swimming around excitedly, looking for any remaining scraps of urchin roe. Take your pick of what is available or move on to the next chum station if you didn't see any fish large enough to spear or you missed your shot.

While chumming is regularly practiced by scuba divers, keep in mind that serious freedivers consider chumming unsportsmanlike.

Strive for a Straight Shot

It's always better when you can shoot a fish so that your spear enters the fish at a right angle to its body rather than at a slant. If the spear enters the fish's body at a slant it must travel through more flesh and you are less likely to have your spear completely penetrate to the other side. Without complete penetration, unless you get a kill shot, there is always the chance that the fish will get away.

The most successful spearfisherman keep their eyes on the fish, not on their gun, when taking aim. They practice instinct shooting rather than trying to "sight" their gun in any way.

Shoot for Where the Fish is Going to Be

Wayne Gretzky, the great hockey player, once said that he doesn't skate to where the puck is, but where the puck is going to be. To spear fish consistently you must aim for where the fish is going to be, not where it is at the moment, unless it isn't moving. Learning how to anticipate a fish's movements is one of the most important skills you can develop as an underwater hunter.

Subdue the Fish at Your First Opportunity

Always be sure to subdue your fish at the first opportunity that you have to get close to it. This is particularly important if you are using a polespear with a paralyzer tip, if you have incomplete penetration of your shaft, if you have speared a fish in a non-vital part, or if you have a fish with soft flesh.

Grab a fish either by the gills, or by the eyes by placing your thumb and forefinger over the eyes and pinching them together. Grabbing a fish by the gill plate won't do much to subdue the fish, but it is one of the few places you can get a firm grip on most fish. You can also pin a fish against the bottom using your spear shaft and run the stringer either through its gills or eye sockets while you hold it against the bottom .

When you pinch a fish by the eyes they will be forced inward in their sockets. Since most fish have a bony skull this will provide a positive finger hold on what is otherwise a round, slippery body. In addition, when you grab a fish by its eyes it momentarily blinds the fish so it can't see and helps to paralyze the fish by placing pressure on certain nerves.

Never grab a fish by placing your hand in its mouth or by its fins. Even fish with relatively small teeth can produce painful bites that can penetrate thin gloves. Dorsal fins (the fins on the fish's back) frequently have sharp spines that can produce puncture wounds that can easily become infected.

With smaller fish, it is usually easy to control the fish and string it by inserting your stringer from one eye socket to the other. This sometimes has the added benefit of piercing the fish's central nervous system, which will almost instantly paralyze the fish. This technique does not work for any of the flatfish, such as the flounders or California halibut, since both their eyes are on the same side of their head.

Another way to subdue your fish once you have a grip on it is to stab it in the brain or sever the fish's spine with a short, sharp knife. With larger fish, you can also rip out the fish's gills which will also bring its struggling to a quick halt, but this isn't as quick as using a knife or stringer properly.

Get the fish on a stringer, in a game bag, or push your shaft completely through the fish and out the other side so the fish is on the gun's line, even if you intend to boat the fish right away. You must have a means of controlling the fish that is positive and secure. Trying to hold a slick, struggling fish with gloved hands is almost impossible and you stand a good chance of losing your catch.

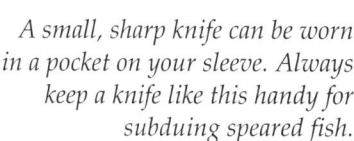

A small, sharp knife can be worn in a pocket on your sleeve. Always keep a knife like this handy for subduing speared fish.

Keep a Log

As you explore different spearfishing sites, be sure to keep a detailed log of your experiences. This will help you to become more successful as time goes by. You want to collect information on dives where you shot fish and on dives where you didn't see fish.

As you accumulate data you will begin to see patterns appear that will help you to know where to go under different conditions and at different times of year. Information that you will want to record will include time of day, visibility, water temperature, depth, currents, bottom conditions, and any other environmental factors that affect what happens.

Developing a Sixth Sense

The best underwater hunters are those who develop a sixth sense about when and where the fish are going to be. Nobody can teach you how to do this; it's either something you have or you don't. If you have it, it can be developed and nurtured, but it can't be taught.

CHAPTER 8

MAXIMIZING YOUR FREEDIVING ABILITIES

In the past few years, spearfishing while freediving has seen a renewed popularity among many divers. There are probably many reasons why this is so, but among them are the following factors:

- Freediving provides a good workout and can be more strenuous than scuba diving. For divers who approach freediving seriously, it can be a great way to stay in shape.

- Freediving allows you to get close to certain fish that you might never be able to approach while using scuba.

- Freediving requires less hassle and equipment than scuba. When you wear less equipment it is easier to swim and move through the water. For divers who have bad backs, freediving removes the weight of the scuba cylinder and usually decreases the amount of weight you need to wear on your weight belt.

- You can generally wear a thinner wetsuit for freediving than what you would need to wear for scuba diving. This gives you increased flexibility, making it easier to swim and dive more comfortably.

- Freediving is less expensive than scuba diving. You don't need the same equipment, nor do you have the expense of filling scuba cylinders or buying batteries for a dive computer. You don't have to deal with the annual inspection of cylinders, annual regulator maintenance, or hydrostatic tests of scuba cylinders.

- Freedivers generally cover more ground and get to see more fish than scuba divers.

- Freedivers generally spend more time in the water on a given day than scuba divers. They are not constrained by the limitations of their breathing gas supply.

In order to get the most out of freediving, and increase your safety, you need to have a good understanding of the physiological effect that breath hold diving has on your body. Freediving affects your heart rate in very different ways than scuba diving. It also has a direct effect on your production of carbon dioxide and your body's use of oxygen.

Some people make the mistake of thinking that since freediving is done without compressed air that it is safer than scuba diving. This is not true. Freediving has certain risks that it holds in common with using scuba as well as risks that are unique to freediving. There have been many freediving accidents and fatalities over the years and you must have a good understanding of what's involved if you want to become a serious freediver.

Some of the ideas in this chapter are equally applicable to scuba diving, so use the information that applies to the way you dive. Equalization, fluid balance, maintaining warmth, and freediving after scuba diving are all topics that are important to scuba divers.

EAR EQUALIZING

To be an effective freediver, your ears and sinuses must clear freely and easily. Where a scuba diver has the luxury of a lengthy air supply and can take his time clearing his ears if they are "sticky", a freediver needs to get down to the bottom with a minimum amount of delay. Every second spent struggling to clear a blocked Eustachian tube is time that is subtracted from your bot-

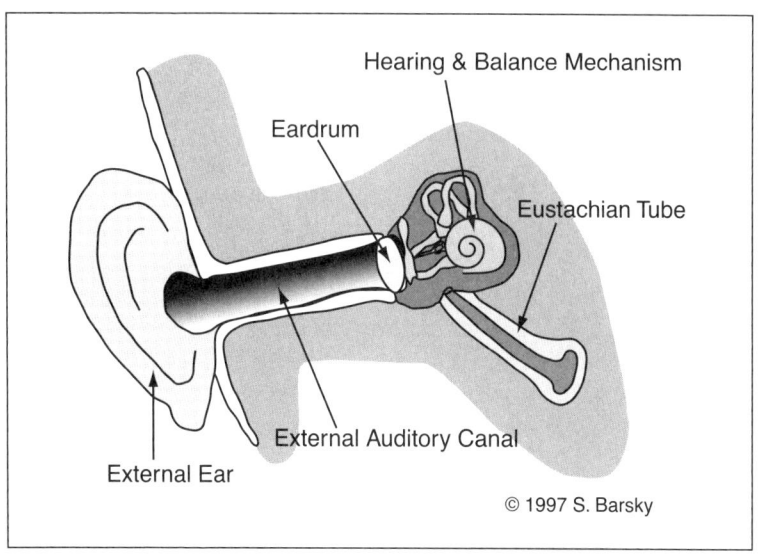

Your ears must equalize easily for freediving.

tom time for hunting. If it takes you ten seconds to clear your ears and you can only hold your breath for one minute, then you have just lost one sixth of your bottom time.

Most scuba divers find that it is much easier to clear their ears when they do a feet first descent, than if they descend head first. The reason for this is that when you descend head first, blood rushes to your head, swelling the tissues there. To be an effective freediver, however, you must be able to descend head first, to get effective propulsion and to avoid wasting time rotating from a head up to a swimming position. For this reason, it is even more essential as a freediver that you start equalizing on the surface, before you descend, and keep equalizing throughout your dive.

If you wait until you feel pressure, or worse – pain, on your eardrum you have waited too long to clear. Keep your Eustachian tubes clear and equalize every few feet, whether you feel the need to clear or not. Blow gently and do not force equalization.

Some divers do not equalize easily under any circumstances, although there seems to be some indication that if you equalize more frequently it becomes easier. If you have a hard time equalizing, freediving may be more difficult for you.

GIVE YOUR BODY TIME TO ACCLIMATIZE TO THE WATER

It takes time for your body to acclimatize to being in the water, especially if the temperature is cold. Don't expect to jump in the water and perform at your best immediately. Allow yourself twenty to thirty minutes for your body to get acclimated to being in the water.

MAMMALIAN DIVING REFLEX

Whenever you perform a dive while holding your breath, your body experiences a distinct physiological response known as the mammalian diving reflex. This response includes a dramatic decrease in your heart beat and a shunting of blood from your arms and legs to your body's core. The purpose of these actions is to provide more oxygen to the vital organs, such as the heart and brain, to ensure their survival while underwater.

All marine mammals exhibit the mammalian diving reflex. These elephant seals can dive to great depths. (© Skip Dunham. All rights reserved.)

All mammals exhibit this response to being submerged, but it is most dramatic in marine mammals, such as whales, dolphins, seals and sea lions. The heart rate drop in these animals is especially pronounced. For example, the elephant seal can dive to depths of up to 2067 feet, while its heart rate drops from a maximum of 120 beats per minute on the surface to an unbelievable 4 beats per minute while submerged! They are able to dive for up to 32 minutes at a time. Wouldn't it be great if we could do the same thing?

The mammalian diving reflex is the main reason why cold water drowning victims can frequently be successfully revived after being submerged with nothing to breathe for extended periods. The body mechanisms of cold water drowning victims shut down to extremely low levels that allow extended survival and rescues, provided that they are carefully rewarmed and resuscitated.

If you can learn to relax underwater, the mammalian diving reflex will help you to achieve a longer bottom time during each dive. If you don't relax, your heart will beat faster and you will use up more oxygen, decreasing your ability to stay underwater.

Blood Shifts

A number of years ago, U.S. Navy diver Bob Croft set several depth records for breath-hold diving. Navy doctors and scientists studied Croft to try to determine why he could achieve the depths that he did. Initially, they could not understand why Croft's lungs did not collapse during his dives. Their confusion was focused on Croft's lung volume, which they thought must be quite high.

The average person has a normal lung volume of not quite two gallons of air. When you breathe normally, however, you don't move all of the air out of your lungs when you exhale. There is still more air that you can exhale if you are forceful. Yet, even when you exhale as strongly as possible, some air still remains in your lungs. This remaining air is known as your "residual volume".

For many years, diving medical specialists believed that if you made a breath-hold dive deeper than the depth where the air in your lungs compressed beyond its residual volume, your lungs would collapse and you would suffer tissue damage. Croft seemed immune to this problem.

The Navy made films of Croft during a series of deep breath-hold dives. When Navy doctors watched the film they came up with a theory that would explain why Croft's lungs didn't collapse. In the films it appeared that Croft's skin became very loose on his body during the dive. They felt that the blood was shifting from his skin to his core, causing the spaces between his lung tissues to fill up with fluid during the dive, much as a sponge soaks up water. Since fluids can't be compressed, this would prevent his lungs from being damaged. If this theory is correct, then it would appear that all breath-hold divers seem to experience this effect to a certain degree during deeper dives.

While there is nothing that you can do to enhance this effect, you should be aware that this is just one of the body's mechanisms that may help you dive underwater.

Shallow Water Blackout

In an attempt to stay underwater longer, many freedivers use the technique known as "hyperventilation" to extend their dive times. This is an extremely dangerous practice and one that has led to numerous diving fatalities.

Hyperventilation is defined as rapid and forceful breathing with an emphasis on exhalation. When you hyperventilate your body lowers its level of carbon dioxide. Carbon dioxide is a waste product of normal respiration (breathing) and is the "trigger" that stimulates you to breathe.

While you can't completely get rid of the carbon dioxide in your body, by hyperventilating you can take it significantly below the normal level. When you do this you can extend your dive time because you don't feel the need to breathe.

The danger from hyperventilating doesn't occur at depth, but occurs near the surface. While you are at depth, the pressure on your body is increased. As you swim and hunt, you consume the oxygen that is in your body. Although the oxygen level in your tissues is falling, while you are at increased pressure there is no noticeable effect due to the increased partial pressure of the oxygen in your system.

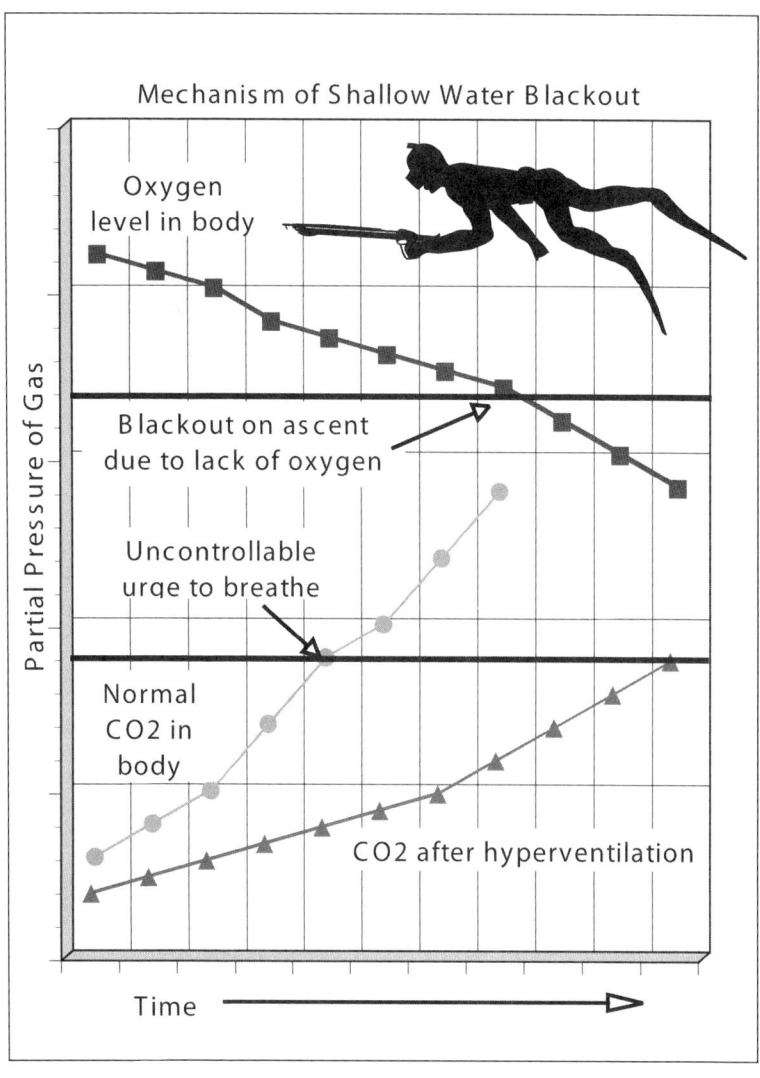

Shallow water blackout is a major hazard for freedivers, as shown in the above chart. As the body consumes oxygen at depth, carbon dioxide is produced. However, following extended hyperventilation, the carbon dioxide level is lowered to the point where a freediver can pass out due to a lack of oxygen without ever feeling the need to breathe. This chart shows how shallow water blackout occurs.

Maximizing Your Freediving Abilities

As you return to the surface, the pressure on your body decreases, and the partial pressure of the oxygen in your tissues also falls. Eventually, you will reach a point where there is insufficient oxygen in your tissues to maintain consciousness. However, if you have hyperventilated you will never feel the need to breathe that one normally does when you hold your breath without hyperventilating. This happens because there is not enough carbon dioxide in your system to trigger the urge to breathe. This type of accident is known as "shallow water blackout".

Many experienced freedivers have died because of shallow water blackout. Divers who have been rescued under these circumstances almost always report that they never felt the urge to breathe and that they don't remember anything about passing out. Almost all divers who suffer this type of accident are quite surprised to learn they were rescued.

Hyperventilation and shallow water blackout are deadly killers. Don't make the mistake of using hyperventilation to extend your breath-hold dives. There is a better way to maximize your bottom time using a technique known as "cycle breathing".

CYCLE BREATHING

Cycle breathing is a technique you can use to extend your breath-hold dive time that allows you to relax in the water, without pushing yourself to the limits of your ability. It is a much better way to train yourself to dive if you want to be a successful breath-hold diver.

Most beginning freedivers try to stay underwater for as long as they possibly can on each dive. When they surface, they are out of breath and it takes them many long minutes to recover to the point where they can comfortably dive again. If something goes wrong while they are underwater, they have nothing in reserve to get themselves out of a problem situation. Holding your breath for as long as possible on each dive is an inefficient way to stay underwater.

Divers who practice cycle breathing strive for a much more relaxed rhythm to their diving. Instead of attempting to make every dive last as long as possible, they start out by making very short dives, usually no more than fifteen or twenty seconds long.

Allow enough time on the surface between breath-hold dives to replenish oxygen and get rid of carbon dioxide. Don't hold your breath to the limit on every dive.

Their goal is to make their bottom time approximately equal to the amount of time they spend on the surface between each dive.

To start out, you might spend forty seconds on the surface and only twenty seconds underwater, gradually extending the time you spend underwater and the time you spend recovering from the dive. For safety, it is recommended that you spend a bit more time on the surface between dives then you do underwater. This gives your body adequate time to wash out any carbon dioxide and replenish its' oxygen.

Most divers find it quite easy to work up to a minute underwater and two minutes on the surface in a short time. If you need to spend a bit longer on the surface between dives that's okay; your goal is to establish a comfortable rhythm for you and everyone's capabilities are different. You should not feel stressed or breathless at the end of a dive, you should feel relaxed. With practice, you should be able to easily work up to spending a minute underwater.

It takes training, good habits, and practice for a person to develop their breath-hold diving skills. Don't be disappointed if your results aren't spectacular the first time you try cycle breathing.

MAINTAINING YOUR BODY TEMPERATURE

To be an effective freediver, it is extremely important to maintain your body core temperature, i.e., the temperature of your chest cavity and internal organs. Even in relatively "warm" water, your core temperature will drop because the water is colder than your core.

As mentioned in the chapter on equipment, in cold water, i.e., waters colder than 70 degrees F, you need a good wetsuit or dry suit, with accessories that include a hood, gloves, and booties. If you fail to protect these vital parts of your anatomy, you cannot maintain your body temperature.

For freediving, most divers use a good quality wetsuit. If all your diving will be scuba diving in cold water, a dry suit is the best way to keep warm. Serious divers who dive year-round often own a dry suit for use in the colder, winter months, and a wet suit for freediving or diving in warmer waters.

If you select a dry suit, keep in mind that they require additional training. You must not dive with a dry suit unless you have been properly trained in its use by an experienced dry suit diving instructor.

When you dive in cold water, your body shuts down the circulation to your arms and legs, in an attempt to maintain your core temperature. This increases the blood volume in your chest and abdominal areas, circulating more blood through your kidneys and increasing the production of urine by your body. Your body loses both heat and moisture when you urinate.

When you are cold, your ability to think clearly is definitely impaired and your coordination is affected as well. These factors taken together make it extremely difficult to squeeze off a good shot at a fish. Maintaining your body temperature is essential.

In addition to having a good wetsuit or dry suit and

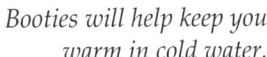

Booties will help keep you warm in cold water.

other accessories, there are other things that you can do to help maintain body warmth. Be sure to get enough rest before you dive, since being fatigued will affect your ability to keep warm. High carbohydrate content foods, such as pasta, eaten the day before you dive will help provide the energy you need. Avoid foods that are high in protein content, such as meat.

Keep in mind that while headlands or "points" that jut out into the ocean are often productive areas to hunt, cold currents that flow around these areas can chill your body more quickly. Diving in a cold, strong current is like walking in a high wind on a cold day. Just as there is a wind chill factor on dry land, a cold, strong current can carry heat away from your body underwater. When possible, get behind rocks or wrecks that are in the path of the current and use them to shelter your body to help maintain warmth.

Cold currents that flow around points can rapidly rob your body of heat.

Before you enter the water, fill your wetsuit with warm water, so you don't have to use the energy from your body to heat up the water that enters your suit. However, don't stand under a hot shower when you come out of the water, unless you are done diving for the day. Exposing your body to a hot shower between dives, allows the capillaries in your skin to re-expand causing you to lose more heat.

Stay out of the wind between dives as this can cause rapid chilling. The wind will cause the water trapped in the nylon on the outside of your suit to quickly evaporate, leading to a high heat loss.

Keep in mind that as your wetsuit ages, the foam neoprene cells inside the suit will begin to break down and lose their insulation value. When this happens, the suit will no longer be as warm as it was when your first bought it, even though outwardly the suit will still appear to be in good condition.

Be sure to rinse your wetsuit thoroughly after diving in salt water. If you fail to do this, the salt crystals that form when the suit dries will cut the cells of the suit and cause it to deteriorate much more rapidly.

Maintaining Fluid Balance

Maintaining your body's fluid balance is extremely important, whether you are freediving or scuba diving. Even in warm water, your body will lose fluids, which will interfere with your performance.

Your body produces a hormone known as "ADH", or Anti-Diuretic Hormone. Whenever you dive, the production of ADH is suppressed and diuresis, the production of urine, occurs. The loss of body fluids through urination is increased whenever you dive in cold water, as previously explained.

Without sufficient body fluids, the transport of oxygen in your body will be poor. Since proper oxygen levels are essential to your freediving capability, you must ensure that you maintain sufficient fluids in your body.

Proper fluid levels are also important in helping scuba divers to avoid decompression sickness. If your body fluid levels are low, you are much more prone to decompression sickness.

To maintain the correct level of fluids in your body be sure to avoid beverages such as coffee, tea, colas, and alcohol. Coffee, tea, and colas all contain caffeine, which increases blood flow and causes a higher production of urine producing fluid loss. Alcohol also inhibits the production of ADH, which as previously explained, helps to prevent fluid loss.

Between dives in cold water drink fluids like herbal teas, hot cocoa, warm sports drinks, and water. In hot weather, drink water, cold sports drinks, and soft drinks without caffeine. Keep your body well hydrated for diving.

Freediving After Scuba Diving

Although there have been no scientific studies on the subject, there have been numerous accidents that seem to indicate that freediving shortly after scuba diving is extremely hazardous. It appears that divers who do aggressive freediving after scuba diving are somewhat prone to blackout underwater. A number of divers have died in accidents of this type.

Another problem with freediving after scuba diving is that if you have a borderline no-decompression situation, repeated breath hold dives could push you into a case of decompression sickness. Each time you free dive, your body absorbs a little bit more nitrogen at depth. This additional nitrogen coupled with the rapid ascents common in freediving could cause nitrogen bubbles to come out of solution in your body, producing decompression sickness.

It is also conceivable that even if you have done no scuba diving in the prior 24 hours, you can accumulate enough nitrogen through repeated breath-hold dives to suffer from decompression sickness. While this is hard to do in cold water, it is a real possibility in warmer water.

Considering these two dangers, underwater blackout and possible decompression sickness, it's best to avoid freediving after scuba diving. The increased risks are not worth the possibility of injury or death.

Notes

Chapter 9

Spearfishing Competition

As mentioned in Chapter 1, spearfishing competition played an important role in the start of modern sport diving. While you don't hear much about it today, competitive spearfishing is still with us, although its popularity is not nearly as great.

Competitive spearfishing is regulated in the United States by the Underwater Society of America (USOA). The USOA is the official United States National Governing Body for Underwater Sports, and is a member of the U.S. Olympic Committee. In addition to spearfishing competition, the USOA sanctions competition in underwater hockey, fin swimming, underwater rugby, and underwater photography.

The USOA is made up of "councils" of diving clubs from different regions all over the country. These councils send their best spearfishermen to participate in national spearfishing competitions that are normally held once each year in various locations.

In Europe and the rest of the world, spearfishing competition falls under the auspices of the Confédération Mondiale des Activité Subaquatiques (CMAS), which translates as the "World Underwater Federation" in English. Spearfishing teams that represent the USOA compete in international spearfishing meets sponsored by the CMAS.

The Underwater Society of America, USOA, is responsible for the organization of competitive spearfishing in the United States.

CMAS, the World Underwater Federation, promotes spearfishing competition on a worldwide basis.

THE REAL COMPETITION STARTS BEFORE THE MEET

Knowing the underwater terrain is essential to successful spearfishing and this is even more true when it comes to competition. Since spearfishing meets are held in different locations all the time, to win a meet you must put in the time to scout the area where the meet will be held to know where to find fish. Because there is no time to do any scouting during competition, you must invest the time prior to the start of the event.

At the national level, local diving guides are usually made available for up to one week prior to the meet to give visiting divers an orientation to the site where the championship will be held. Those divers who know where to find the fish are usually the winners.

Knowing where to find the big fish is essential to winning a competitive meet.

RULES FOR COMPETITION

The rules for spearfishing competition change, both in the U.S. and abroad, so keep in mind that what you read here will undoubtedly be somewhat different in years to come. I have included only those rules that are essential to an understanding of the essence of spearfishing competition, i.e., rules that pertain to the diving and equipment, rather than the judging, protests, or mechanics or organizing and running a spearfishing meet. I have also included the rules that I feel are least likely to change.

• *All competitive spearfishing is done while freediving. No scuba diving is allowed.*

This rule has been a standard of spearfishing competition since the beginning. It is unlikely this rule will change.

• *The equipment that may be used for diving includes:*

Snorkel, mask, knife, fins, suit, weight belt, spearguns, inflation type life preserver, floats and hardware, and other minor accessories.

• *Only foot fins may be used for propulsion while in the water.*

No scooters allowed!

• *Only muscle-loaded spearguns or spears may be used.*

Band guns, polespears, and pneumatic guns all fit this description. Guns fired through the use of gunpowder or other mechanisms are prohibited.

• *Competitors must be at least 15 years of age.*

The age requirement could go up or down, but the point is that there is a minimum age required to compete, but no maximum age.

• *Competitors can be disqualified for using alcohol and/or drugs, unsporting conduct, a disregard for safety, or the use of oxygen.*

The reason oxygen is not allowed in competition is that by breathing pure oxygen, you can greatly extend your breath-holding time. This is an extremely risky practice because breathing pure oxygen prior to making a breath-hold dive washes carbon dioxide out of your body more effectively than hyperventilation. This makes the risk of shallow water blackout even greater.

• *Each competitor must have a valid fishing license.*

Of course they must also obey all local fishing regulations.

• *At the national level, competition is a team effort.*

These teams are usually composed of not more than three divers. Team members can assist each other in landing speared fish.

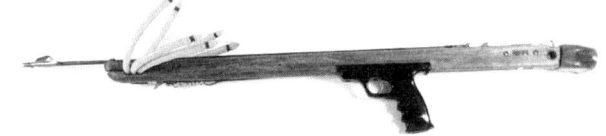

Only muscle-loaded spearguns or spears may be used in competition.

• *No electronic equipment (i.e., GPS, Loran, etc.) may be used on the day of the meet.*

The competition is based on the participant's topside and underwater navigational skills.

• *Chumming is not legal.*

Although chumming is an accepted technique for recreational spearfishing, it is recognized as giving the diver an advantage during competition and is thus prohibited.

• *Meets usually last not less than four hours and not more than six hours on any given day.*

National and international events typically last for one or two days.

SCORING AT SPEARFISHING COMPETITIONS

Most spearfishing competitions at the time of this writing have been scored on the basis of the number of fish taken and the total weight of the fish taken. The speared fish from the event are given to charitable organizations. Although no fish is wasted, this intense hunting pressure places extreme short term pressure on the resources of the section of ocean or lake where the event takes place.

It seems likely that spearfishing competition may change in the future to follow the pattern established by the Long Beach (California) Neptunes Dive Club which hosts an annual Blue Water Meet. The policy of the Neptunes is to only allow participants to take one fish and the largest fish of the meet wins the competition. Each underwater hunter is expected to take his catch home to eat it himself.

CHAPTER 10

THE FUTURE OF SPEARFISHING

Spearfishing is one of the most satisfying diving activities that a diver can pursue. It takes a combination of watermanship, knowledge of the ocean, knowledge of marine life, and intuition to be able to consistently bring home dinner. Yet, the best spearfishermen are always content to bring home nothing more than a memory and will even let a large fish swim away when the mood strikes them.

In the future there may be new spearguns that use more sophisticated means of propulsion, but the basic elements of the sport will remain the same. You can enjoy spearfishing with the simplest polespear or with the most sophisticated pneumatic gun. No matter which device you choose, the results will still come down to your ability to go underwater and meet the fish on its own terms.

The most serious threat to spearfishing will come from man's own greed and the inability of some divers to take just enough fish for their immediate family's consumption. If we are not careful, we can destroy the resources of the ocean. If we are prudent, there will be fish to hunt for our grandchildren.

I wish you safe diving and good hunting.

APPENDIX I

SCIENTIFIC NAMES

Scientific names are organized by the following divisions:

Kingdom - Plants versus animals. Fish are animals so they are in the kingdom *Animalia*.

Phylum - The next division separates animals with backbones from animals without backbones. Fish have backbones so they are in the phylum *Chordata*.

Class - Most fish that you will hunt will probably be bony fishes in the class *Osteichthyes*, rather than sharks, which are cartilaginous, and belong to the class *Chondrichthyes*.

Order - Once you reach this level, you are beginning to reach a more specific division of types of fish. At this level, the animals will be more similar to each other.

Family - At the family level, the animals will have a very similar shape and appearance.

Genus - A genus is a group that is made up of several closely related species.

Species - This is the most specific classification used for identifying each type of fish from the next. Fish of the same species are all related by "blood" and can mate with fish of the opposite sex.

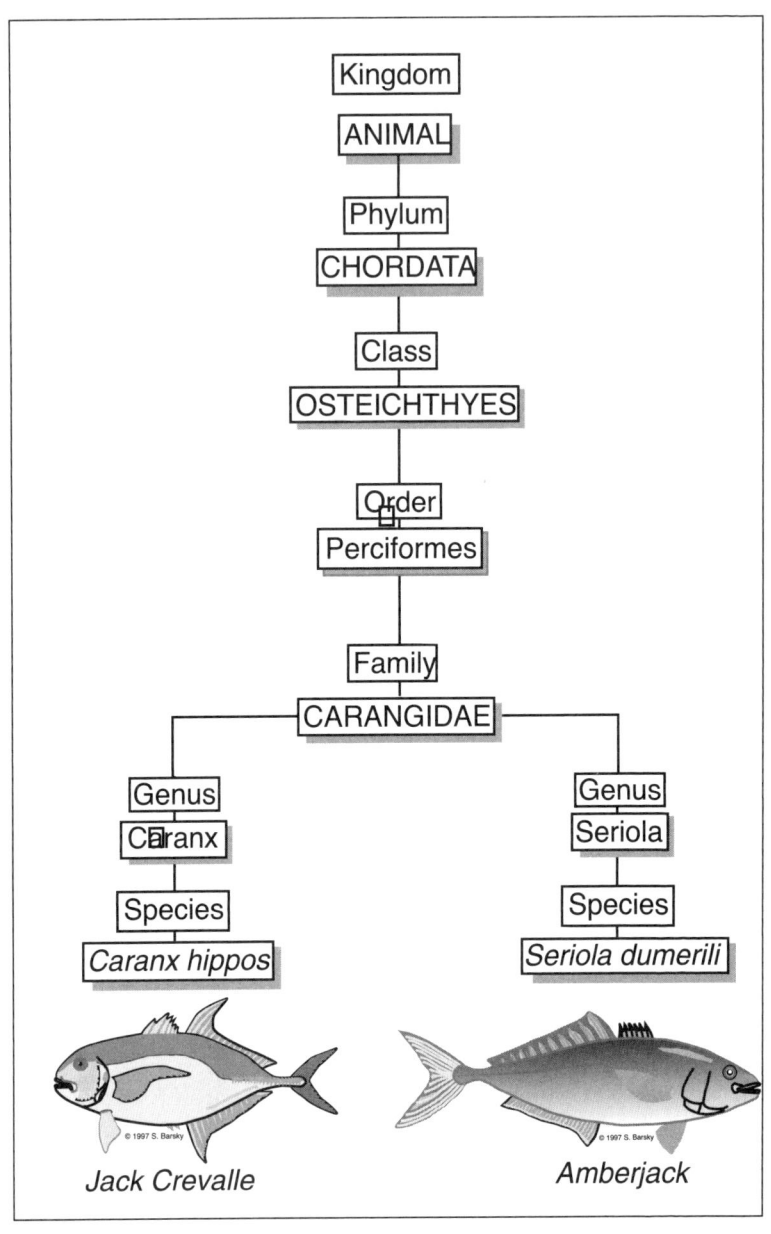

This chart shows how a fish is classified down to the species level.

When a scientific name is given it is normally given by the genus name, followed by the species name. The names are all in Latin, although frequently part of the name may reflect the name of the person who discovered the animal.

For example, the California halibut's scientific name is *Paralicthys californicus*. The genus name is *Paralicthys*, while the species name is *californicus*. Even though they are somewhat similar in appearance, the Pacific halibut, *Hippoglossus stenolepis*, is a very different species that is entirely unrelated to the California halibut. They are not even considered to be in the same family.

By contrast, rockfish all belong to the same family, *Scorpaenidae*, and many are so similar they belong to the same genus, *Sebastes*. The difference between individual species may come down to such seemingly trivial matters as the number of spines along the dorsal fin or the number of scales along the side.

Scientists use what is known as a "*key*" to determine which fish they are examining. In most cases, a key will actually be a book devoted to a particular class of animals in a particular region. The key describes the differences in anatomy from fish to fish in minute detail. By following a key properly, it is possible to distinguish between animals that are very similar in appearance.

Recommended Reading

Books on Fish

Eschmeyer, W. and Herald, E. *A Field Guide to Pacific Coast Fishes of North America*, Houghton Mifflin Co., Boston, MA 1983

Gotshall, D. *Pacific Coast Inshore Fishes*. Sea Challengers, Monterey, CA, 1981

Kaplan, E. *A Field Guide to Coral Reefs*. Houghton Mifflin Co., Boston, MA, 1982

Miller, D., and Lea, R. *Guide to the Coastal Marine Fishes of California. Fish Bulletin 157*. State of California, Department of Fish and Game. Sacramento, CA, 1972

Robins, R., and Ray, C. A *Field Guide to Atlantic Coast Fishes of North America*. Houghton Mifflin Co., Boston, MA, 1986

Snyderman, M. and Wiseman, C. *Guide to Marine Life: Caribbean, Bahamas, Florida*. Aqua Quest Publications, Locust Valley, NY, 1996

Books on Spearfishing

Eyles, C. *Last of the Blue Water Hunters*, Watersport Publishing, San Diego, CA, 1991

Gilpatrick, G. *The Compleat Goggler*, Dodd Mead and Co., New York, NY, 1957 (Out of print)

Maas, T. *Blue Water Hunting and Freediving*, BlueWater Freedivers, Ventura, CA, 1995

Sheckler, D. *Successful Underwater Hunting*, St. Brendan Co., Torrance, CA, 1994

About the Author

Steve Barsky has been scuba diving for many years. He is experienced in sport, scientific, and commercial diving, and is an avid underwater hunter and photographer.

Steve started diving in 1965 in Los Angeles County and bought his first speargun at the age of 15. He became a NAUI instructor in 1970. His first employment in the industry was with a dive store in Los Angeles, and he went on to work for almost 10 years in the retail dive store environment.

He attended the University of California at Santa Barbara, where he earned a Masters Degree in 1976 in Human Factors Engineering. His masters thesis was one of the first to deal with the use of underwater video systems in commercial diving. Steve's work was a pioneering effort at the time and was used by the Navy in developing applications for underwater video systems.

Steve Barsky is a professional underwater photographer and author.
(© Bob Evans, La Mer Bleu Productions)

Steve traveled to the North Sea in 1976 and worked as a commercial diver through 1983. He made dives from drill rigs, supply ships, and barges throughout the North Sea, Gulf of Mexico, and along the east coast of the U.S.

In 1983, Steve returned to Santa Barbara to work for Diving Systems International, a manufacturer of commercial diving masks and helmets. He worked in marketing for Diving Systems, producing all of the company's manuals, catalogs, and advertisements.

Barsky was marketing manager for Viking America, Inc., an international manufacturer of dry suits from 1986-1988.

In 1989, Steve formed Marine Marketing and Consulting, based in Santa Barbara, California. The company provides market research, marketing plans, consulting, newsletters, promotional articles, technical manuals, and other services for the diving and ocean industry. Steve also does diving accident investigation and serves as an expert witness in diving accident litigation.

Steve is an accomplished underwater photographer. His photos have been used in numerous magazine articles, catalogs, advertisements, training programs, and textbooks. As a writer, Barsky's work has been published in *Sea Technology, Underwater USA, Skindiver, Offshore Magazine, Emergency, Fire Engineering, Dive Training Magazine, Searchlines, Sources, Undersea Biomedical Reports, Santa Barbara Magazine, Selling Scuba, Scuba Times, Sport Diver, Underwater Magazine, Scuba Diver*, and many other publications.

Steve is a co-author of *Careers in Diving*, with his wife Kristine and Ronnie Damico, and *Small Boat Diving*, also published by Best Publishing. He is also the author of *Diving in High Risk Environments*, published by Dive Rescue International. He is a joint author with Dick Long and Bob Stinton of *Dry Suit Diving: A Guide to Diving Dry*, published by Watersport Books. He has taught numerous workshops on contaminated water diving, dry suits, and other diving topics.

Steve lives in Santa Barbara, California where he regularly dives the Channel Islands with his wife Kristine, a marine biologist.

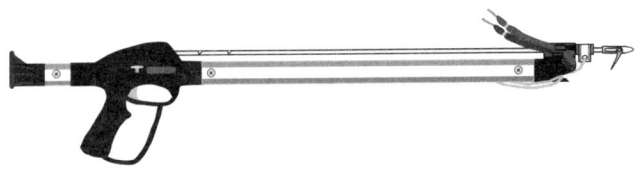

INDEX

.22 caliber cartridges 3
6 inch adjustable wrench 52
Abalone 89
Abalone shell 28
Accessories 32, 35-36
Accident 33, 70, 72, 122
Acclimatize 124
Accuracy 25, 30, 32, 40
ADH 132
Aiming 25
Air 53, 68, 70
Air powered horns 50
Alaska 87, 89, 91, 96
Alcohol 132, 137
Alexander 28
Aluminum 13, 44
Aluminum barrels 21
Aluminum tubing 19
Amber surgical tubing 41
Amberjack (*Seriola*) 69, 98, 101
. . . . 100,113
Ambush feeders 79
Ammunition 40
Anacapa Island 84, 85
Anadromous fishes 64, 83
Anal opening 102
Anatomy 143
Anchoring 72
Anchovies 79, 81, 96
Animal rights activists 8
Animalia 141
Ankle weights 57
Anti-Diuretic Hormone 132
Arbalete 18
Arm 49
Arm strength 4
Artificial rock reefs 67
Atractoscion nobilis 95
Attached hood 59
Bacteria 102

Bag limit 8
Bahamas 1
Bait-fish 113
Baja California 84, 87, 89, 92
Balistidae 94
Ballast 72
Band powered gun 11, 18, 22
Bands 18, 20-21, 24, 26-27, 40-41
Barbs 37
Barnacles 42, 70
Barracuda 94, 98
Barrel 11, 18, 32, 45
Batteries 122
Bays 110
Beach 108
Bermuda 86
Beuchat 54-55
Biologists 77
Bite 79
Black sea bass (*Stereolepis gigas*)
. . . . 85-86
Blackout 133
Blood 102, 126, 130
Blood vessel 102
Blue Water Hunter 25, 45
Bluewater hunters 75
Bluewater hunting 69
Boat 63, 65, 108, 110
Boat handlers 72
Boat traffic 71
Bob Evans Design/Force Fins® 55
Body cavity 102
Body mechanisms 125
Body size 4
Body temperature 130
Body's core 124
Bones 51
Boots 59
Bottom 71, 110, 118
Bottom conditions 120

Index   147

Bottom fish. 116
Bottom time 65, 123
Bowline. 42
Braided nylon 42
Brain 119, 124
Brass snap hook. 48
Brazil. 81, 100
Breakaway gear. 45
Breakwaters. 92
Breath-hold dive 55, 128
Breath-hold divers 126
Breath-hold diving skills 129
Breathing 55
Breathing gas supply 122
Bridges 80
British Columbia. 87
Broomtail grouper (*Mycteroperca xenarcha*) 86
Bubbles. 114
Buckle 61
Buoyancy 22, 32, 45, 58, 116
Buoyancy compensator 49, 73, 114
Butt 18, 24
Cabezon (*Scorpaenicthys marmoratus*) 89
Cables 72
Caffeine. 133
Calico bass (*Paralabrax clathratus*)
. . . . 67, 84, 85, 112
California 63-64, 82, 84, 86, 91
California Dept. of Fish and Game. . 85
California halibut (*Paralicthys californicus*) 65, 78-81, 119, 143
California sheephead (*Semicossyphus pulcher*) . . . 91, 92, 117
Canopy 68
Cape Hatteras 77
Capillaries 131
Carangidae. 98
Carbohydrate. 131
Carbon dioxide 122, 126, 129, 137
Caribbean waters 75
Carp, (*Cyprinus carpio*) 76, 77
Catch regulations 76
Catfish. 64
Cathodic protection 72
Cave. 65-66, 70
Cave diver training. 66
Cave diving etiquette. 66
Cave diving techniques 66

Caverns 65-66
Chandleries 107
Channel Islands. 79, 96
Charitable organizations 138
Chest. 60
Chest cavity 130
Chondrichthyes 141
Chordata. 141
Chumming. 117, 138
Ciguaterra 94, 98, 101
Citation. 106
Clams 92
Class 141
Cleaning stations. 87
CO_2 cartridges. 3
CO_2 powered gun. 3
Coast Guard. 72
Cobia (Rachycentron canadum) 83
Cocking pad. 24, 60
Cod (Gadus morhua) 77, 78
Coffee 132
Colas 132
Cold water drowning. 125
Coloration 90
Commercial trawlers 91
Common name 76
Compartments. 70
Competition 136-137
Competitive spearfishermen. 28
Compressed air 6, 29, 122
Compression 61
Concrete structures. 67
Confédération Mondiale des Activité Subaquatiques (CMAS) 135
Consciousness. 128
Conservation 4, 6-8
Convenience 13
Copper rockfish. 91
Coral reefs. 46, 63-64, 68, 69
Core temperature 130
Cork. 39
Corn starch. 59
Corrosion inhibitor 20
Corrugated hose 55
Coryphaenidae 89
Cost 32
Councils 135
Counter-shading. 101
Cousteau, Jacques. 1
Coves 110

Crabs	83, 91
Creek	63, 80
Cressi Sub	54, 55
Crevalle Jack	99
Crevices	65, 69, 84
Croft, Bob	125
Crowds	108
Crustaceans	78, 80, 90, 92
Curiosity	113
Currents	49, 65, 110, 111, 120, 131
Custom guns	28
Cycle breathing	128
Dacor	55
Dagger	49
Danger	70
Dealer	33
Death	94, 133
Decompression sickness	132-133
Deep drop-offs	68, 107
Deep reefs	69
Defensive weapon	40
Depth	65, 120
Depth compensated belt	61
Desalination	72
Detachable spearheads	37, 38
Determination	5
Diarrhea	94
Direct sunlight	65
Dive club	2, 135
Dive computer	122
Dive gear	63
Dive logs	74
Dive stores	107
Dive-Alert™	50
Diving fatalities	70, 126
Diving guides	136
Diving Pioneers	2
Dolphin (*Coryphaena hippurus*)	69, 89-90, 125
Dolphins	125
Dorsal fin	90, 119
Dorsal spine	95
Downward angle	110
Drag	53, 55, 110
Drugs	137
Dry suit	66, 130
Ears	122
Eggs	63
Electric shock	71-72
Electronic equipment	138
Elephant seal	125
Endangered species	64
Endurance	5
Engine cooling	72
Entanglement	44, 71
Entrapment	69
Entry point	110
Equalization	122-123
Esclapez	55
Estuaries	78, 80
Europe	29, 135
Eustachian tube	122, 123
Exhalation	126
Experience	15
Experienced divers	72
Extra Force Fin®	56
Eye sockets	118
Eyes	48, 80, 110, 118
Falling objects	71, 73
Family	83, 141
Family *Labridae* (Wrasses)	91
Farallon Islands	47
Farmer john style pants	60
Fastex® buckles	57
Fatalities	122
Feet first descent	123
Fiberglass	13
File	15, 39, 51
Fillet	103
Fillet knife	49
Fin swimming	135
Fin weights	57-58
Fines	63
Fins	18, 57, 109, 116, 119, 137
Firearm	21, 30, 105
Firing pin	40
Fish and game authorities	103
Fish blood	103
Fish boxes	103
Fish identification books	75
Fish poisoning, also see ciguarterra	94
Fish species	63
Fish stocks	8
Fishing laws	6, 8
Fishing violation	106
Fishing watches	107
Fit	53
Flares	50
Flashlight	46, 65-66, 84
Flat blade screwdriver	52

Flatfish 65, 110
Flesh 49, 88-89, 96-97, 118
Flexibility 13, 58, 121
Float lines 43
Floats 28
Florida 81-82
Flounder 106, 116, 119
Fluid balance 122, 132
Food 1, 110
Foot 32, 60
Foreign matter 30
Four barb head 35
France 2, 18
Freedive 44
Freedivers 56, 97-98, 115, 117
Freediving 53-54, 58, 115
. . . . 121-122, 133, 137
Freedom of movement 58
Fresh fish 4-5
Fresh water 63, 75
Freshwater lakes 77
Full foot fins 56
Game bag 119
Game warden 63, 76
Gas bubbles 3
Genus 76, 141, 143
Gig heads 35-36
Gill plate 79
Gill rakers 79
Gills 48, 79, 102, 118-119
Gilpatrick, Guy 2
Gloves 14, 26, 32, 59, 79
Gobies 87
Goggles 1, 53
Goody bag 103
Gopher rockfish 91
Government agencies 72
GPS 138
Grass rockfish 91
Gravity 110
Great barracuda
 (*Sphyraena barracuda*) 96
Greater amberjack
 (*Seriola dumerili*) 100
Grip 26
Groupers 95
Grunion 107
Guide tube 11
Gulf Coast 82
Gulf of Mexico 43, 86, 94, 102

Gun bag 45
Gun barrels 19
Gun designers 22
Gut shot 7
Habitat 63-64, 66, 70, 75, 108
Habits 75
Hair conditioner 59
Halibut 15, 67, 108, 110, 112, 116
Hanauers, Eric 2
Handle 22, 32
Hawaii 94, 102
Hawaiian sling 11-12, 15
Hazards 69, 71-72, 74
Head 59, 110
Headlands 131
Heart 125
Heart beat 124
Heart rate 125
Herbal teas 132
Hexagrammidae 87
High tide 80, 106
High waisted pants 60
Hip 24
Hog snapper 93
Hogfish
 (*Lachnolaimus maximus*) 93, 94
Holding power 35-36
Holes 65, 69, 84
Honeycomb cell surface 58
Hooks 73
Humboldt Bay 86
Hunting pressure 138
Hunting techniques 65
Hydrostatic tests 122
Hyperventilation 126, 128
Ice 103
Impact 13
Impulse® snorkel 54
Incoming tide 106
Indians 7
Inflatable buoy 45
Inflatable tubes 50
Initial run 43
Injury 26, 133
Instinct shooting 25, 118
Instructor 71
Insulation 60
Intended target 27
Internal complexity 32
Internal mechanism 29

Internal organs 102, 130
Internal seals 33
Introduced species 77
Intuition 139
Invertebrates. 70, 100-101
Islands. 63
Jack crevalle (*Caranx hippos*) . . . 99, 100
Jack mackerel. 101
Jacket. 60
Jam. 21
Juvenile fish 6
Kelp. 14, 48, 68, 111
Kelp bass 84
Kelp forests 63-64, 67-68, 84
Kelp rockfish 91
Kevlar®. 42
Key 143
Kidneys. 130
Kill shot 15, 118
Kinesthetic sense. 116
Kingdom 141
Kingfish 101
Knife 28, 48, 73, 98, 102
. . . . 117, 119, 137
Knife pocket. 60
Lakes. 64
Larvae. 63
Latin 76
Law 63
Leaks. 33
Leg. 49
Legal responsibility 76
Legal size 7
Lethal weapons 21, 30, 40, 105
Liability problems. 71
Lift. 70
Line 43, 66
Line pack 22, 28
Line release mechanism. 18, 23, 27
Lingcod (*Ophiodon elongatus*). . . . 87-89
Live boat. 72
Live electrical current. 72
Loader. 32
Local fishing regulations
. . . . 63, 69, 76, 78, 115
Location 65
Loctite® 222 Small Screw
Threadlocker 37, 51
Log. 120

Long Beach (California) Neptunes
Dive Club. 138
Long blade fins 53, 55
Loss of habitat 8
Low tide 106
Low volume masks. 53
Lower back. 57
Lucayans 1
Lungs 53, 126
Mackerel. 96
Magdalena Bay 79, 96
Mahi-mahi 89
Maintenance. 15, 27, 32
Mammalian diving reflex. 124-125
Man-made structures 64
Manufacturer 22, 32-33
Map. 74
Mares. 29, 54
Marine creatures 69
Marine environment. 50
Marine growth. 43
Marine life 65, 139
Marine mammals 125
Mask 26, 53-54, 137
Massachusetts 83, 100
Matches. 51
Maximum power 25
Measuring lines. 106
Measuring tape 106
Memory 139
Mexico 85, 96
Mid-handle guns. 22
Modification. 37
Mollusks. 78, 92
Monofilament 48, 73
Monterey, California 92
Moon. 107
Moral decision. 9
Morality 6
Motor 49
Muddy bottoms. 64, 80
Multi-barb heads. 35, 37
Mussels. 70, 117
Muzzle 18, 20, 22, 42
Narrow blade knife. 48
Nassau grouper (*Ephiephelus striatus*)
. . . . 86-87
Native American Indians. 6
Nausea 94

Index 151

Navy doctors 125
Neoprene 132
Nerves....................... 119
Nest.......................... 89
Night..................... 46, 93
Nitrogen 133
Noise 61, 108, 114-116
Non-native species 77
North Carolina 86
Nose 53
Nova Scotia 92
Numbness 94
Nutrients 110
Nylon line.................. 24, 41
O-ring seals 29, 38
Ocean Master................... 55
Oceanic........................ 55
Oceans........................ 75
Octopus.................... 88-89
Offshore oil platforms.... 43, 70-72, 99
Oil 29, 33
Oil company 71, 72
Oil spill 72
Ono 101
Open muzzle 20
Open season.................... 7
Open water 74
Order......................... 141
Oregon 64, 82
Orientation................... 136
Orr, Glenn 2
Outgoing tide.................. 106
Owner's manual 31
Oxygen 122, 125, 129, 132, 137
Oysters 92
Pacific amberjack
  (*Seriola colburni*).............. 100
Pain......................... 123
Palos Verdes Peninsula 85
Paralichthys californicus............ 143
Paralyzer tips.......... 14, 35, 36, 118
Parasites 87
Partial pressure 128
Patterns...................... 120
Peacock flounder (*Bothus lunatus*)
  .... 65, 81-82
Pelagic fish 69, 75, 91, 108
Penetrating ability................ 35
Penetration............ 13, 38, 40, 118
Percicthyidae 82

Personal injury 32, 40
Phillips head screwdriver 52
Phylum 141
Physiological response........... 124
Physique....................... 59
Picasso 55
Piers.......................... 80
Pike 64
Pilings........................ 92
Pinnacle 111
Pipelines...................... 72
Piston 29, 32
Plastic foam 106
Plastic frame 53
Plastic sheath 39
Plastic tubing................... 43
Pliers......................... 52
Pneumatic gun 3, 11, 29-30, 32-33
  .... 60, 137, 139
Points of land.................. 110
Polespear.............. 11, 13-14, 15
  .... 26, 35, 106, 118, 137
Polynesia 1, 11
Poor visibility 12
Positive image 8
Potts, Wally 2
Power 32, 41
Power inflator 114
Power/length ratio............... 32
Powerheads 40
Pre-fabricated cast concrete........ 67
Precautionary decompression stop 116
Predator 47, 53
Preferred depth range 84
Pressure 31, 33
Prey 79
Private fishing boats.............. 73
Prodenovich, Jack 2
Protein 131
Pump.......................... 31
Purists........................ 53
Push-rod mechanism 22
Queen triggerfish (*Balistes vetula*)... 95
Range 15, 105
Rays.......................... 83
Rebreathers 114
Recoil 22, 26
Reef 21, 49
Reel 22, 42-44
Refillable cylinder 3

152   Spearfishing

Regulations 75	Scientists. 125
Regulator maintenance 122	*Scombridae*. 101
Release mechanism. 44	Scooters. 137
Relief. 66	*Scorpaenidae* 143
Reloading 26	Scuba. 121
Repairs 32	Scuba cylinder 121, 122
Residual volume 125	Scuba diver 61, 80, 92, 94-95
Resort destinations 69	. . . . 97, 114-115, 117, 123, 132
Resources 6, 8	Scuba diving 53, 58, 95, 133
Respiration. 126	Scuba Tuba™ 50
Rhythm 128-129	Scubapro. 2
Riffe 18, 20, 28, 40-41	Sea Bear 29
Ring. 37	Sea buoys 83
Risks 122, 133	Sea lion 125
River 63, 64, 78	Sea urchin. 66, 93, 117
Rock. 46	Sea water 72
Rock points 39	Seagrass beds. 87
Rock reef. 63, 67, 75, 84, 99, 107	Seals 60, 125
Rockfish (*genus Sebastes*) 67, 83, 90	*Sebastes* 143
. . . . 91, 143	Selective hunter. 6
Rocks. 14, 21, 39, 42, 51, 111	Separate lenses 53
Rocky bottoms 64-65, 67, 78, 92	*Serranidae* 84
Roe. 89	Sexual reproductive capacity 6
Rope 73	Shadow. 116
"Rough" fish 64	Shaft. 12, 14, 18, 20-22
Rubber sling. 15	. . . . 24-25, 30, 32, 41, 66, 84, 119
Rubber weight belts 61	Shallow water blackout 128
Rubble. 67	Sharks 40, 47, 69, 83, 97, 103
Rules for Competition 136	Sharpening steel 51
Safety 23, 32, 137	Sharpening stone. 39
Safety factor 61	Sheath 60
Safety mechanisms 20	Sheephead 93
Salmon 64	Shelf-life 50
Salt. 132	Shellfish 117
Salt water 72	Shipwrecks. 69, 78, 83
San Clemente Island 85	Shock. 13
San Diego 2	Shock cord 23, 42
San Francisco Bay 86	Shocking power. 35
Sand 30	Shooter booties 56
Sand bottom 64-65, 67, 78, 94	Shore. 65
Santa Barbara. 85, 98	Shower 131
Santa Cruz 85	Shrimp. 83, 90-91, 100
Sardines 79, 96	Shunting of blood 124
Saturday Evening Post. 2	Side cutters. 52, 73
Scales. 39, 93	Signaling device 49
Scallops. 48	Single barb heads 35
Schools 92, 96	Single sided nylon. 58
Sciaenidae (Croakers). 95	Sinuses 122
Scientific literature 76	Sixth sense 120
Scientific name. 76, 143	Size limit. 7

Index

Skill	5
Skin	69
Skin Diver Magazine	2
"Skin in" rubber	60
Skull	49
Skyblazer® flares	50
Slide	18, 23, 42
Slip tip	38, 96
SMG	3
Snap hooks	52
Snap swivels	37
Snorkel	53, 54, 115, 137
Soft drinks	133
Soft flesh	35-36, 38
Sound signaling devices	50
South Carolina	92
Spares	39
Spawn	81
Spawning aggregations	87
Spawning season	78
Spear	118
Spear shaft	11, 40
Spear tip	35, 39, 96
Spearfishermen	48, 75, 78, 96
Spearfishing competition	135
Speargun	11, 13, 26, 29, 35, 46, 68-69, 105-106, 137, 139
Speargun line	100
Spearheads	39
Spears by Riedel, Inc.	13
Species	76, 141
Species name	143
Sphyraenidae	96
Spinal shot	79
Spine	49, 79, 110, 119
Spines	119
Spirotechnique	18
Sporasub	54
Sports drinks	132
Sportsmanlike attitude	115
Spring	78, 82
Spring powered spear guns	3
Squid	65, 79-80, 83, 88-90, 96, 112
Squid hounds	83
Stainless steel	19, 40, 44
Stainless steel mirrors	50-51
Stainless steel wire	38, 43, 48, 73
Stalking techniques	6
Starfish	70
Steel hulls	69
Steelhead trout	64
Stiletto	49
Stopping power	26
Storage	33
Storm	68
Stream	63, 78
Streamlining	114
Strength to weight ratio	42
Stringer	44, 46-47, 68, 119
Striped bass (*Morone saxatalis*)	82-83
Structural cross members	71
Struggling fish	47
Stud guns	3
Sub Marine Gun	3
Submerged trees	64
Suction	53
Suction pipes	71-72
Suit	137
Summer	78, 80, 82
Summer flounder (*Paralicthys dentatus*)	80
Sun	116
Surface	57-58
Surface dives for freedivers	116
Surface float	43
Surgical tubing	12, 14, 18, 41
Swaging tool	51
Swivels	52
Synthetic rubber	41
Tackle	73
Take-down polespears	13
Talcum powder	58
Tank	61
Tapmatic Corp.	3
Target	36, 106
Tautog (*Tautoga onitis*)	91
Tea	132
Teak	19, 28
Teeth	79, 95, 119
Temperate water	67
Temperature	92, 111, 112
Tension	19, 25
Terminal boredom	65
Terrain features	74
The Compleat Goggler	2
Thermocline	84, 112
Thigh	32, 60
Thin blades	49
Three pronged head	14
Thrill of the hunt	4, 6

Tides 80, 106	Vital organs 60, 124
Time 120	Voit Swimaster 2
Tingling of the lips 94	Vomiting. 94
Tip 15, 20, 32, 37, 43	Wahoo (*Acanthocybium solanderi*)
Tissue damage. 126	. . . . 69, 75, 101-102
Torpedo buoy 43	Waist seal 60
Toxin. 98	Washington 64
Transition zone 107	Water. 132
Trident 35	Water movement. 60
Trigger 18-19, 23, 25-26, 28, 40, 42	Water temperature 78, 120
Triggerfish (*Bulistes*) 94	Watermanship. 139
Trophy fish. 83	Waterproof coating. 40
Tuna 69, 75	Watersports enthusiasts. 2
Tuna line. 42	WD-40® 20, 52
Tunnels. 69	Weight 53, 61, 116, 121
TUSA. 55	Weight belt. 49, 58, 121, 137
Twin barb spear tips. 36	Weight belt buckle 24, 60
U.S. Divers Co., Inc. 54	West coast 15
U.S. Olympic Committee. 135	Wetsuit. 53, 59, 66, 111, 121, 130
Underbelly 102	Wetsuit socks. 56
Underwater habitats. 11	Whales 125
Underwater photography 135	Whistles 50
Underwater rugby 135	White nylon 42
Underwater Society of America	White seabass 6, 28, 38, 67, 95-96
(USOA). 135	White sharks 47
Underwater terrain. 107, 111	Wind 49, 132
United States 29, 77	Wire cutters 73
United States National Governing	Wire rope swage fittings 51
Body for Underwater Sports 135	Wishbone 19, 24, 25, 41
Upper annular valve. 54	Wooden guns. 19
Urchin roe 117	World Underwater Federation 135
Urine. 132	Worms 78, 80, 97
Ventral fins. 92	Wreck 46, 49, 63, 70, 92, 97
Vermillion rockfish. 91	Yellowtail (*Seriola dorsalis*) 6, 28
Visibility 27, 64, 110, 120	. . . . 69, 98-99, 113
Visual devices 50	Zinc anodes 72